Praise for Brian Leaf's *Top 50 Skills* Series

D0406208

Top 50 Skills for a Top Score: SAT Math

"What a surprise, what a relief! An SAT guide that actually meets you where you are, talks to you with wit and compassion, and clears away the panic of test-taking. And, the writing is first-rate too. Bravo, Brian Leaf."

Rebecca Pepper Sinkler, former Editor, *The New York Times Book Review*

"I enjoyed the informal writing style, and the flash cards for math are brilliant! Students are used to stacks of vocabulary words in preparation for the verbal portion of the test, why not drills on flash cards for the math section?"

Denise Brown-Allen, Ed.D., Upper School Director, The Pingry School

"If everyone starts using Brian's secrets and strategies, The College Board and ETS are going to have to rewrite the SAT!!"

Max Shelton, George Washington University, Class of 2012

Top 50 Skills for a Top Score: SAT Critical Reading and Writing

"Brian Leaf has hacked off the head of America's high school boogie man—the dreaded SAT. He clearly lays out how the test works, accessible preparation strategies, and how to maximize one's score. Any college applicant can benefit from his thoughtful and well-researched advice."

Joie Jager-Hyman, former Assistant Director of Admissions, Dartmouth College, author of *Fat Envelope Frenzy: One Year, Five Promising Students, and the Pursuit of the Ivy League Prize*

"A long time ago, in an era far, far away, I took the SAT—and I can remember the pressure and anxiety of it like it was yesterday. Lucky for you modern-day seniors, Brian Leaf has written the SAT guide to end all SAT guides. He thoroughly demystifies the test and lays out the 50 skills you need to max out your score. Better yet, Mr. Leaf writes with such humor, wit, and unpretentious expertise that you'll find yourself reading this book just for fun. I did. It almost—almost—even made me want to take the SAT again."

Sora Song, Senior Editor, *Time Magazine*

"What's more scary than facing SATs? Or more boring than prepping for them? For a student swinging wildly between angst and ennui, the solution is Brian Leaf's *Top 50 Skills for a Top Score: SAT Critical Reading and Writing*. Leaf, himself a genius at connecting with teenagers, meets students at their level, and spikes every drill with common sense and comedy. I especially loved the Superbad Vocabulary section—not your usual stuffy approach to language deficit disorder. Guaranteed to relax and engage the most reluctant (or panicked) student."

Rebecca Pepper Sinkler, former Editor, *The New York Times Book Review*

Top 50 Skills for a Top Score: ACT Math

"Anyone even thinking of taking the ACT needs this short but targeted guide to the math section. You simply can't afford not to spend the time reading his laser-sharp drills that break down every type of problem on the ACT, show the math behind each type, and then provide drill sections based on that skill set. Even poor math students can learn to recognize all the types of math on the ACT and learn the ropes enough to get most of the easy and medium questions right every time. Mr. Leaf's guide is even entertaining as he gives the skill sets names like "Green Circle, Black Diamond" to make it feel like you are skiing rather than slogging through lessons. If you want a short but concise guide to the ACT with every trick and mathematical explanation necessary to get a perfect score, this is the book for you. You may even actually LEARN real math in the process as Mr. Leaf's love of the subject shines through so you don't just feel you are learning for a test."

Dr. Michele Hernandez, author of the bestselling books *A is for Admission, The Middle School Years,* **and** *Acing the College Application*

"Brian Leaf knows how to talk with students and in his book, *Top 50 Skills for a Top Score: ACT Math,* you can hear his voice loud and clear. Students who follow Brian's 'Mantras' and work through the practice questions will gain confidence in their work, as well as improve their ACT scores."

Barbara Anastos, former Director, Monmouth Academy

"Feels like you have an insider divulging secrets from behind the walls of the ACT! At times going so far as to circumvent the math skills themselves, Brian gives practical tips and tricks specifically designed to outwit the ACT's formula, and he does it all with a sense of humor and fun. Nice job!"

Danica McKellar, actress (*The Wonder Years, West Wing***) and mathematician and author of** *New York Times* **bestsellers** *Math Doesn't Suck* **and** *Kiss My Math*

Top 50 Skills for a Top Score: ACT English, Reading, and Science

"This book is a good read even if you *don't* have to take the ACT."

Edward Fiske, author of the bestselling college guide, the *Fiske Guide to Colleges*

"The **specific** skills needed for the ACT, confidence building, stress-management, how to avoid careless errors . . . this book has it covered!"

Laura Frey, Director of College Counseling, Vermont Academy, and former President, New England Association for College Admission Counseling

McGraw-Hill Education
Top 50 Skills for a Top Score

McGraw-Hill Education
Top 50 Skills for a Top Score:
SAT* Reading, Writing & Language

Brian Leaf, MA

New York | Chicago | San Francisco | Athens | London | Madrid |
Mexico City | Milan | New Delhi | Singapore | Sydney | Toronto

Copyright © 2017, 2010 by Brian Leaf. All rights reserved. Printed in the United
States of America. Except as permitted under the United States Copyright Act of
1976, no part of this publication may be reproduced or distributed in any form or
by any means, or stored in a database or retrieval system, without the prior
written permission of the Publisher.

1 2 3 4 5 6 7 8 9   ROV   21 20 19 18 17 16

ISBN   978-1-2595-8565-4
MHID   1-2595-8565-4

e-ISBN   978-1-2595-8566-1
e-MHID   1-2595-8566-2

SAT is a registered trademark of the College Entrance Examination Board, which
was not involved in the production of, and does not endorse, this product.

McGraw-Hill Education products are available at special quantity discounts to use
as premiums and sales promotions, or for use in corporate training programs.
To contact a representative, please visit Contact Us pages at
www.mhprofessional.com.

Contents

How to Use This Book

It's simple. The questions that will appear on your SAT are predictable and in this book I will teach you exactly what you need to know. I will introduce each topic and follow it with drills. After each set of drills, check your answers. Read and reread the solutions until they make sense. They are designed to simulate one-on-one tutoring, as if I'm sitting right there with you. Reread the solutions until you could teach them to a friend. In fact, do that! My students call it "learning to channel their inner Brian Leaf." There is no better way to learn and master a concept than to teach it!

Any new concept or question type that you master will be worth 10 or more points toward your SAT score. That's the plan; it is that simple.

This book is filled with SAT Reading/Writing Mantras. They tell you what to do and when to do it. This is the stuff that Paula, who got perfect 800s, does automatically. The Mantras teach you how to think like her.

"Sounds good, but the SAT is tricky," you say. It is, but we know their tricks. Imagine a football team that has great plays, but only a few of them. We would watch films and study those plays. No matter how tricky they were, we would learn them, expect them, and beat them. SAT prep works the same way. You will learn the strategies, expect the SAT's tricks, and raise your score. Now, go learn and rack up the points!

Guessing

The SAT is not graded like an English test at school. If you got only half the questions right on your sophomore year English final, that'd be a big fat F. On the SAT, half the questions right is about a 500, the average score for students across the country. If you got 75 percent of the questions right, that'd be a C in school, but almost a 600 on the SAT, the average score for admission to schools like Goucher and the University of Vermont. And 89 percent correct, which is a B+ in school, is a beautiful 700 on the SAT, and about the average for students who got into Georgetown, U.C. Berkeley, Emory, and Wesleyan.

Use the above information to determine how many questions you need correct on the SAT. Easy questions are worth just as much as hard ones, so don't rush and risk careless errors on questions that appear easy just to reach the harder ones. When a question seems hard, take another look for what you are missing. Ask yourself, "Which skill can I use? What is the easy way to do this question?" After you complete this book, you will know!

What about guessing? Well, you do not lose points for wrong answers, so put an answer for every question, even ones that you do not get to. Even if you are running out of time at question 40 out of 44, budget a bit of time to fill in an answer for the last 4 questions. It'd be crazy not to. Statistically, if you randomly fill in the last four ovals, you'll get one correct. That could be worth 10 points on your score! So keep an eye on the clock, and when there are a few minutes left, choose an answer for each remaining question. Of course, when you have completed this book, you'll understand the test, you'll work faster and yet get more correct, and you'll rarely need to guess!

About Brian Leaf, MA

Six, maybe seven, people in the world know the SAT like Brian Leaf. Most are under surveillance in Princeton, NJ. Brian alone is left to bring you this book.

Brian has seen the SAT from every angle, even teaching yoga to the test makers at ETS Corporation. You are about to find out what Brian learned from them while they slept in deep relaxation.

Brian is the author of McGraw-Hill Education *Top 50 Skills* SAT and ACT test-prep series. He is also the author of *Defining Twilight: Vocabulary Workbook for Unlocking the SAT, ACT, GED, and SSAT* (Wiley, 2009). Brian is Director of the New Leaf Learning Center in western Massachusetts. He teaches SAT, PSAT, and ACT prep to thousands of students from throughout the United States. (For more information, visit his website www.BrianLeaf.com.) Brian also works with the Georgetown University Office of Undergraduate Admissions as an Alumni Interviewer.

For more about Brian, check out his hilarious memoir, *Misadventures of a Garden State Yogi.*

Acknowledgments

Special thanks to all the students of New Leaf Learning Center for allowing me to find this book. Thanks to my agent, Linda Roghaar, and my editor at McGraw-Education, Anya Kozorez. Thanks to Pam Weber-Leaf for great editing tips, Zach Nelson for sage marketing advice, Ian Curtis for assiduous proofreading, Kyle Rodd for his encyclopedic vocabulary, Manny and Susan Leaf for everything, and of course, thanks most of all to Gwen, Noah, and Benji for time, love, support, and, in the case of Noah and Benji, rejuvenating ninja-battle breaks.

Thanks also to the following individuals who generously allowed me to use their work as reading and essay passages: Tavi Wolfwood (Pretest Essay Passage and Essay Skills), Sarah Duggan (Essay Skills), The Coen Brothers (Skills 18 and 21), Emma Sakson (Pretest), Kyle Tucker (Writing the Perfect 12 Essay), David Rice (Pretest, Posttest III, Skill 15), Ian Curtis (Skills 17 and 23, Writing the Perfect 12 Essay), Colette Husemoller (Skill 14, How to Read, Skill 20, Posttest III), Noah Dirks (Skill 37), Alex Milne (Essay Skills, Posttest I), Manpriya Samra (Skill 13: Drill 2), and Danielle Keith (Posttest II).

Pretest

This pretest contains questions that correspond to our 50 Skills. Take the test, and then check your answers in the 50 Skill sections that follow.

> *Each passage or pair of passages below is followed by a number of questions. After reading each passage or pair, choose the best answer to each question based on what is <u>stated</u> or <u>implied</u> in the passage or passages and in any accompanying graphics (such as a table or graph).*

The following passages consider the roles of two leaders of a group of plane crash survivors on an island.

Passage 1

Transformed by the plane crash and reborn on the island, John Locke is the true leader of the survivors of Oceanic 815. Once paralyzed and struggling with inner and outer demons, Locke
5   stood up from the crash on the beach and was able to walk. This physical epiphany restored his faith in people and changed his philosophy on life completely. This "man of faith" leads his fellow survivors on the path that saved him—
10 the path of the island. Now a strong believer in the power of the island, Locke knows that the place where they are stranded has a purpose for everyone. Following the will of the island, Locke guides others who are lost as he once
15 was, showing them hope for the future and a chance to start anew.

Passage 2

From the moment Oceanic Flight 815 crashes into the island, Dr. Jack Shepherd secures his position as the preeminent leader of the group
20 of survivors. A successful surgeon with a troubled history, Jack is a man based on principles and fact, giving his fellow survivors a sense of realistic optimism and security during a time of

confusion and chaos. With a heavy emphasis on
25 logic and reason, Jack avoids hokey mysticism. Confronted by the mysterious and inexplicable challenges that the island presents him with, he shows his leadership qualities in the democratic decisions that he makes in the best interest of
30 the group and for the ultimate goal of getting everyone rescued.

(handwritten annotations: "what make him a leader", "involves people", "qualities of leader", "who he is")

1

1 The passages share the common aim of

(A) telling the story of the crash of Flight 815.

(B) analyzing the anatomy of a leader.

(C) describing the path of the island.

(D) identifying the leader on the island.

2 The primary purpose of Passage 2 is to

(A) tell the story of Oceanic Flight 815.

(B) demonstrate why Jack Shepherd is the true leader of the survivors.

(C) profile the personality of Jack Shepherd.

(D) examine the theme of challenge.

3 In Passage 1, line 13, "will" most nearly means

(A) testament.

(B) stubbornness.

(C) being.

(D) desire.

4 Passage 2 indicates that the principle to which Shepherd is most loyal is

(A) leadership.

(B) optimism.

(C) chaos.

(D) reason.

5 The two passages suggest that a leader must do all of the following EXCEPT

(A) inspire followers.

(B) govern democratically.

(C) provide hope.

(D) have faith in others.

6 In lines 13 to 16, the author of Passage 1 makes the assumption that

(A) the survivors want to start anew as John Locke did.

(B) John Locke was once paralyzed.

(C) John Locke feels no hope.

(D) Jack Shepherd was a successful surgeon.

7 The author of Passage 1 would most likely regard Dr. Jack Shepherd with

(A) absolute puzzlement.

(B) unabashed contempt.

(C) amusement.

(D) qualified disapproval.

8 The author of Passage 2 would most likely regard John Locke with

(A) reverence.

(B) indifference.

(C) skepticism.

(D) caustic abhorrence.

This passage is adapted from a film review written in 2006.

The most distinctly American of all genres, the Western has evolved and changed greatly over the past sixty years. After an initial "rebirth" marked by John Ford's *Stagecoach*, the genre's
5 moral conflicts and dominant ideologies have grown ever more complicated. We can see this progression in the contrast between the gloomy and existentially aimless *Dead Man* (1995) and the relatively idealistic and naïve *Stagecoach*
10 (1939). From one to the other, the myth of pure masculinity has become convoluted, the male hero less omnipotent, the not always moral White settler less a symbol of "Family Values," and America less of a pristine, idealized dream.
15 However, both films still adhere to some defining genre conventions, both aesthetically and thematically, so some aspects remain the same.

A close examination of the following points will be adequate to illustrate this change. We shall
20 see what form the roles and portrayals of Indians, women, white civilization, violence, and the hero's masculinity and mission take in each film. In the time between *Stagecoach* and *Dead Man*, encompassing the bulk of WWII and the
25 entirety of the war in Vietnam, each category has grown progressively darker and less supportive of an idealized notion of "America the Beautiful." Jim Jarmusch's *Dead Man*, featuring an effete, nearly-albino Johnny Depp as a
30 banker named William Blake, is part of a larger trend that aims to besmirch a long-established Western legend that *Stagecoach* unambiguously supports. As the Western serves largely to present a certain image of this country's foundations
35 and of the men who laid them, these changes are significant not only within the film, but also as they serve to redefine film's role in society.

The table shows examples of Westerns released and their gross revenue in each of four sample years.

	1939	1981	1995	2010
Sample Westerns	Stage-coach	The Lone Ranger	Dead Man	True Grit
Gross Revenue (in millions)	$0.297	$12	$1	$171

9 The passage is best described as

(A) an illustration of an ongoing relationship.

(B) an introduction to a character.

(C) a social commentary on the Western genre.

(D) a nostalgic depiction of a Western hero.

10 Which choice provides the best evidence for the answer to the previous question?

(A) lines 1–2 ("The . . . years")

(B) lines 10–17 ("From . . . same")

(C) lines 18–19 ("A . . . change")

(D) lines 23–28 ("In . . . Beautiful")

11 Based on the table and the passage, which film best captures the Western genre?

(A) *Stagecoach*

(B) *Dead Man*

(C) *True Grit*

(D) The passage and the table do not indicate which film best captures the Western genre.

12 In line 13, the quotation marks around the words "Family Values" serve to

(A) criticize the Western genre.

(B) indicate an irony in the meaning of the words.

(C) emphasize the uniqueness of the author's writing.

(D) support the common use of the words.

13 Which statement about Westerns, if true, detracts most from the author's assertions expressed in lines 15 to 18 ("both films . . . same")?

(A) Both films have a similar style.

(B) Both films examine the theme of love and loss.

(C) *Dead Man* and *Stagecoach* each stick to predictable Western patterns.

(D) *Dead Man* and *Stagecoach* examine different subject matter.

14 In line 19, "this change" refers to

(A) the beginning and end of the Vietnam War.

(B) the different representations depicted in the two films.

(C) the loss of American values.

(D) the changing role of film in society.

Each passage below is accompanied by a number of questions. For some questions, you will consider how the passage might be revised to improve the expression of ideas. For other questions, you will consider how the passage might be edited to correct errors in sentence structure, usage, or punctuation. A passage or a question may be accompanied by one or more graphics (such as a table or graph) that you will consider as you make revising and editing decisions.

Some questions will direct you to an underlined portion of a passage. Other questions will direct you to a location in a passage or ask you to think about the passage as a whole.

After reading each passage, choose the answer to each question that most effectively improves the quality of writing in the passage or that makes the passage conform to the conventions of standard written English. Many questions include a "NO CHANGE" option. Choose that option if you think the best choice is to leave the relevant portion of the passage as it is.

It was a Monday morning in 2006, and I <u>am</u> Kyle
                                        15
Tucker, the politician and intellectual, the defiant liberal embarking on his first day of what would be an illustrious political career. I, with several other interns, <u>were arriving</u> at the "Bermuda Govern-
                    16
ment Offices." We entered the lobby, dispensing automatic "good mornings" and "hellos" (and the occasional "what's up," reserved for the younger, more friendly looking politicians). I approached the bulletin board that held <u>your</u> summer destiny.
                                      17
Jostling amongst other eager students, my eyes read the dreadful words "Kyle Tucker—Assistant to the Assistant to the Assistant Secretary of Security Services."

   "No, No, No!" I thought. <u>Nevertheless.</u> I got
                              18
angry—blood rushed to my head and my knees went weak. I considered protesting, having a tantrum, and <u>I considered quitting.</u> What were
                            19

15 Ⓐ NO CHANGE
   Ⓑ was
   Ⓒ were
   Ⓓ have been

16 Ⓐ NO CHANGE
   Ⓑ had been arrived
   Ⓒ was arriving
   Ⓓ were being arriving

17 Ⓐ NO CHANGE
   Ⓑ one's
   Ⓒ my
   Ⓓ whose

18 Ⓐ NO CHANGE
   Ⓑ But,
   Ⓒ Still
   Ⓓ OMIT the underlined portion.

19 Ⓐ NO CHANGE
   Ⓑ I just plain considered quitting
   Ⓒ quitting
   Ⓓ considering quitting

they thinking? My skills were far stronger than the guy who got the job I wanted. My dreams
20
of valiantly arguing the righteous cause in Parliament were evaporating before my eyes. Not me, the budding politician, an assistant to the assis-
21
tant to the assistant? Rage manifested within me. I was no subordinate. Besides, I hated filing and data entry. I was a politician!

I found my department and I was immediately
22
given a list of mundane tasks. My thoughts went between two poles: the government in serious need of fixing, and the humiliation of filing. I was young, but I understood every aspect in the government.
23

My emotions went from anger to embarrassment to sadness, then back to anger. At some point before midday, I began thinking seriously about quitting. "The Assistant's office, its right
24
downstairs," I thought. But I feared the words "I'll never quit." I feared the gossip ". . . that Tucker kid quit his job . . . looooser." I saw my mom's eyes and heard both of my uncles' laughter.
25
I was on page two of the Fire Station Monthly Expenditures data form when I cracked. What I said to my neighbor intern who worked next to me.
26

20. (A) NO CHANGE
    (B) that guy
    (C) the other guy
    (D) those of the guy who got the job I wanted

21. (A) NO CHANGE
    (B) me the budding politician an
    (C) me the budding politician an,
    (D) me the budding politician; an

22. Which of the following alternatives to the underlined portion would NOT be acceptable?
    (A) department: and I was
    (B) department; I was
    (C) department and was
    (D) department. I was

23. (A) NO CHANGE
    (B) the government offered
    (C) of the government
    (D) for the government

24. (A) NO CHANGE
    (B) office; its
    (C) office, it's
    (D) office

25. (A) NO CHANGE
    (B) moms eyes and heard both of my uncles
    (C) mom's eyes and heard both of my uncle's
    (D) mom's eyes and heard both of my uncles

26. (A) NO CHANGE
    (B) neighbor intern next to me,
    (C) neighbor intern
    (D) neighbor, the intern next to me

I don't recall. Something like, "Bathroom . . . I'll be quick . . . sorry." Climbing the metal stairs, the intern supervisor's cubicle was two flights up.
                                    27

I remember staring at the man sitting there expectantly, the curiously look on his face, and
                        28
then down at my hands, then at the Ministry exit doors. I tried to will myself toward the glass doors. "Now," I thought. But I couldn't.
              29

Freedom was just twenty quick steps away, but I couldn't do it. I turned and walked back down the hall.
30

31 And so I continued my work, and I learned

27 (A) NO CHANGE
    (B) the cubicle of the intern supervisor
    (C) I made a beeline to the intern supervisor's cubicle which
    (D) the intern supervisors cubicle which

28 (A) NO CHANGE
    (B) quizzical
    (C) stormy
    (D) questionable

29 If the writer were to delete the underlined sentence, the paragraph would lose

    (A) an important detail.
    (B) a transition from one sentence to the next.
    (C) some of its personal tone.
    (D) nothing at all, since this sentence is out of place.

30 The writer wishes to add details that emphasize his trip back to his filing. Which would best accomplish this?

    (A) hall, down the harsh metal stairs, straight to the Filing Room, then to my filing.
    (B) hall, feeling the approval of my family.
    (C) hall, knowing that one day I would do more than just file.
    (D) hall, once again angry, yet perhaps more humble.

31 Suppose the writer had been assigned to write a brief essay about internship opportunities in Bermuda. Would this essay fulfill the assignment?

    (A) Yes, because the essay describes his reaction to his assignment.
    (B) Yes, because the essay indicates the effect of internships on young people in Bermuda.
    (C) No, because the essay restricts its focus to the writer's internship experience.
    (D) No, because the essay does not describe how the writer learned from his internship.

a lot that summer. Now I worked content, happy to
                              _____
                                   32
be learning. From now on, hard work I would do.
                          _____
                                   33
It turned out I didn't know everything. I knew
barely anything of Bermuda's government. 34
All I had known of local politics to that point had
been gleaned from my parents' political banter,
lopsided as it was.
_____
       35

32
Ⓐ NO CHANGE
Ⓑ contentedly
Ⓒ in content
Ⓓ with contentedly

33
Ⓐ NO CHANGE
Ⓑ hard would be done by me
Ⓒ hard work is what I did
Ⓓ I would work hard.

34 Which of the following is the best way to revise
and combine the sentences reproduced below?

It turned out I didn't know everything. I knew
barely anything of Bermuda's government.

Ⓐ NO CHANGE
Ⓑ It turned out I didn't know everything,
   I knew barely anything of Bermuda's
   government.
Ⓒ It turned out I didn't know everything, in
   fact I knew barely anything of Bermuda's
   government.
Ⓓ It turned out I didn't know everything;
   and knew barely anything of Bermuda's
   government.

35
Ⓐ NO CHANGE
Ⓑ lopsided
Ⓒ lopsided as the banter was being
Ⓓ lopsided as it's.

Skills 36 to 50: Essay

See Essay prompt on next page.

Bonus Question:

The night before the test, you should

Ⓐ stay up all night studying.
Ⓑ spend time with your most freaked out
   grade-mongering friends.
Ⓒ get answers from someone who is 18 hours
   ahead in Australia and already took the test.
Ⓓ have a nice dinner, relax, and go to bed at a
   reasonable hour.

Essay

Time: 50 minutes

As you read the passage below, consider how the author uses:

- Evidence, such as facts or examples, to support his claims.
- Reasoning to develop his ideas and to connect claims and evidence.
- Stylistic or persuasive elements, such as word choice or appeals to emotion, to add power to the ideas expressed.

Adapted from Aza Lev, *"Cape Cod: The Threat to the Beauty."* Originally published March 1, 2016.

The wind rustles through the sawtooth grass atop the dunes of sand, causing them to dance gently back and forth. It whips through the sand at my feet, churning up a miniature sandstorm and settling into miniscule waves of golden dust: a thousand deserts lined up the sea. The sparkling waters of the Cape Cod Bay creep up and cover my toes, delivering an icy shock in the warm breeze of a summer afternoon.

Since the end of the 19th century, the beaches of Cape Cod have been a beloved home and vacation area to people from all around the United States. Cape Cod has served as the epicenter of cod fishing, it is a nautical landmark and historic port, and it is a buzzing hub of tourism and cultural activity in Eastern Massachusetts. The beaches, nearby towns, fishing and culture have attracted more than 500,000 satisfied visitors every year.

Cape Cod is one of the most beautiful and unique places on earth. The National Park service states that Cape Cod serves as a safe haven for "over 450 species of amphibians, reptiles, fish, birds, and mammals, and a myriad of invertebrate animals." A gorgeous reminder of the beauty of the eastern coastal waters, and a stunning natural refuge, I come here year after year, enjoying the wind, the sun, the water and the sand, but my children may never experience the serenity of this beach.

The beaches of Cape Cod are severely threatened. According to the Massachusetts Office of Coastal Zone Management, 65%–70% of the Massachusetts coastline, particularly in Cape Cod, is eroding and 11% of the Massachusetts shoreline is considered to be "critically eroding." In fact, the Cape Cod shoreline is retreating by between three and thirteen feet per year. For our children to retain the wondrous beauty and tranquility of this place, something must be done.

To fully address this problem and save this precious area, we must first understand the causation of the issue. Coastal erosion in the Cape Cod area results from two primary factors: improper beach care and a rise in global sea levels. Luckily for the future of the beaches, we can have an impact on both of these issues.

The first issue requires a change in consciousness. Tourists are woefully unaware of the very real threat facing the beaches and ignore public and environmental protection laws set up to prevent people from stepping on sand dunes and sand cliffs. As these laws are set up to protect these vital elements of the beach from erosion, it would take only a campaign to inform beachgoers of their vital role.

Then we must target the second and more difficult issue, rising sea levels. Ocean levels are rising due to global warming and the increased melting of ice into the oceanic systems. During the past 100 years, ocean levels have risen four to eight inches. Right now, each year in Cape Cod alone, we lose 65 acres of our beaches and coastal land.

What can you and I do to save these beaches, these cultural landmarks and wildlife refuges? In order to truly make a difference in maintaining and preserving this land, we must reduce carbon emissions and greenhouse gas emissions. We can switch more and more to alternative energies, like solar or wind power. We can renew and recommit to our efforts to in recycling and composting. Even small contributions, like turning off our lights when they are going unused, can make the difference that we need to protect this beautiful sanctuary for our children to enjoy.

Write an essay in which you explain how the author builds an argument to persuade his audience that we need to save the beaches of Cape Cod. In your essay, analyze how the author uses one or more of the features listed in the box above (or features of your own choice) to strengthen the logic and persuasiveness of his argument. Be sure that your analysis focuses on the most relevant features of the passage.

Reading Comprehension

Many students believe that reading comprehension questions are tricky, with several answers that work. But in the next 14 Skills, I'll show you that they're not tricky—in fact, they're totally predictable. In English class, you might spend 30 minutes discussing what Walt Whitman meant when he wrote something, but on the SAT, there can be only one right answer: no tricks, no debate. The reading passage will always provide clear proof of the correct answer. Your goal is to be a detective or a lawyer and find the proof. After learning these 14 Skills, most students enjoy the reading section; it becomes easy and predictable. Read, learn, and drill these Skills, and you'll raise your score, guaranteed!

The Intro Paragraph

Each reading passage is preceded by an introductory paragraph. Many students say, "I just skip those paragraphs to save time," but that material can be very useful. Read these paragraphs carefully. Sometimes they give away lots of info; sometimes they even give us the main idea of the passage. I love this strategy; I love little changes like this that make a big difference. Reading the intro paragraph can help you better understand the passage, which will help you to stay focused while you read and to get more questions right! (This is also a great strategy when you're reading your high school history text or your future college philosophy books; the intro sentences or italics can tell you a lot.)

Here's an example:

This passage is from a memoir published in 2001. The author is a young boy in 1941 who has just emigrated with his family to the United States.

What do we learn from this? A lot. The book is a memoir, a story from the author's life. It took place in 1941, so we wonder if there are references to World War II. The author was new to the United States. Knowing all this will help us with the main idea and tone questions, and it will help us stay focused as we read.

Let's try this out on the intro paragraph from the Pretest.

The following passages consider the roles of two leaders of a group of plane crash survivors on an island.

1. The passages share the common aim of

    (A) telling the story of the crash of Flight 815.
    (B) analyzing the anatomy of a leader.
    (C) describing the path of the island.
    (D) identifying the leader on the island.

Solution: In this case, the short intro paragraph pretty much gives us the answer to the first question. It tells us that the passages "consider the roles of two leaders . . . ." The plane crash and the survivors are important, but the "roles of the two leaders" are the primary purpose. Thus, the best answer is choice D. Choice B is about leadership, but the passage does not analyze what makes someone a leader in general; it analyzes who is the leader on the island. This also brings up an incredibly important point. If you're a J. J. Abrams fan or if you follow old television shows, you may be an expert on *Lost*, able to quote entire episodes and argue complex hypotheses, but you must answer a critical reading question using only the evidence in the passage, not from your outside knowledge. That's why I chose *Lost*: to demonstrate this point, and, well, because it's fun.

Correct answer: D

SAT Reading/Writing Mantra #1
Always begin a reading passage by reading the intro paragraph.

Intro Paragraph Drills

Each of the following is an intro paragraph to an SAT reading passage. What can you conclude from each?

1 Passage 1 was adapted from a 1976 article about environmentalism. Passage 2 was adapted from a 2005 analysis of the environmental movement of the 1970s.

① environmentalism
② two passages
③ take place in 1970s
④ they are analyses

2 This passage was excerpted from a novel published in 1985. As the passage begins, three women are discussing their relationships.

① take place in 1985
② taken from a novel
③ literature passage
④ 3 female characters
⑤ discussing relationships

3 This passage is taken from a 1995 article by a doctor describing new medical technologies available in certain hospitals.

① science passage
② takes place in 1995
③ medicine
④ medical advancements
⑤ new tech in certain hospitals

4 In 1973, the U.S. Supreme Court case *Roe v. Wade*, a landmark case legalizing abortion, sparked tremendous debate. Each of the passages below was written in 1974.

① takes place in 1973-1974
② history/social studies
③ US supreme court
④ dual passage
⑤ conflicting views on abortion

5 This passage is taken from an English novel written in 1820. Mr. Peabody works in Mrs. Primberly's shop. He desires to court Mrs. Primberly's only daughter, Josephine.

① takes place on/before 1820 in England
② literature passage
③ 3 characters
④ marriage
   ↳ court: asking permission to date w/ the intention of marriage

6 In the following passage from a book written in 2005, a music historian discusses changes brought about by CDs and MP3 players.

① literature or science
② takes place in 2005
③ changes taking place
④ compare and contrast (CDs + MP3)
⑤ history of music

The SAT Reading Meditation

After you have digested the short introductory paragraph, read the passage in a relaxed, yet very focused way. This is like meditating. When you notice your mind wandering, come back to the moment; bring your mind back to the reading. Anytime your mind wanders, bring it back. That will save time and energy and bring you closer to being a Zen master. For years, Zen monks in the mountains of Japan have been training with SAT reading passages.

Don't try to memorize details. Read to figure out the main idea and tone—what the passage is about and how the author or narrator feels about it. You don't need to memorize details because almost every detail question on the SAT tells you what line to look at. And when you look back, you'll know what question you're trying to answer, making it even easier to understand what you're reading and find the best answer.

Also, and this is huge, I give you permission not to reread hard lines or lines that you spaced out on. This is especially important for perfectionists. Either you won't need the lines and the time you spend rereading them would have been wasted, or you will need them, but you'll reread them later, knowing the question and knowing what to look for. You will never need any one particular sentence to get the main idea and the tone. The main idea and the tone are expressed throughout the passage.

One more thing. Many students worry, "Can I read this whole passage? It'll take 10 minutes." I actually remember being 16 years old and preparing for the SAT and thinking the exact same thing. Then one day I was like, "Wait, this is ridiculous; how long can it take?" So I timed myself. It took like 2.5 minutes! Try it, and you'll see. Even for a slow reader, reading the passage takes only a few minutes, especially if you use my "Don't Reread Strategy."

Let's take a look at the next question from the Pretest.

2. The primary purpose of Passage 2 is to

  (A) tell the story of Oceanic Flight 815.
  (B) demonstrate why Jack Shepherd is the true leader of the survivors.
  (C) profile the personality of Jack Shepherd.
  (D) examine the theme of challenge.

Solution: As we discussed in Skill 1, the intro paragraph told us the main idea. Plus, the passage continually expresses its purpose: to demonstrate that "Jack Shepherd is the true leader of the survivors." Use the process of elimination; the passage does express the ideas mentioned in the other choices, but choice B is the **primary** purpose.

Correct answer: B

SAT Reading/Writing Mantra #2
Read the passage, looking for the main idea and the tone. That helps you stay focused. Keep asking yourself, "What are the main idea and the tone?" Don't try to memorize details, and don't reread hard lines. If you need them, you'll reread them later when you know the question and what to look for.

The SAT Reading Meditation Drills

What are the main idea and tone of each passage?

Drill 1

The following passage was adapted from a 1998 essay written by a psychology graduate student exploring his heritage.

While my mother's parents spent their lives in New York, my paternal grandparents were born and raised in neighboring villages of Austria. My grandfather's father owned a liquor store and was very religious. My grandfather was the academic of the family. He completed high school, college, and graduate degrees. He worked as a teacher and principal, much more respected positions then than now. I connected deeply with this grandfather, Herman. He and I are sensitive, loving, prone to worry, and innately talented teachers.

relationship/similarity

Though my grandparents and great-grandparents were born in Austria, I am not Austrian. This, I believe, is the case for many Jews in the United States. Belonging to this religion is a cultural heritage as well as a faith. Though I rarely think of myself as Jewish and pay small heed to the holidays, Judaism is a large part of my identity.

What is the main idea?

How does the author or narrator feel about that?

psych

Drill 2

MI

The question of whether law is simply a series of rigid prescriptions and maneuvers or a system with an overarching theme of justice and mercy fuels political, social, and legal discourse. For the Western tradition, the relation between fairness and legal reasoning goes back to the ancient Greeks. In *The Statesman*, Plato recognized that legal universalities cannot be considered under every imaginable circumstance and situation.

Aristotle developed this line of thinking in the *Nicomachean Ethics*, arguing that when circumstantial particulars disrupt a universal mandate, then it is only right to modify the law to ensure equitability. Anything written in universal language will, by its nature, create some exception. Aristotle relayed that equity superseded purely legal justice in the sense that the value of equity went beyond even that of the written law. Aristotle did not create a framework for carrying out his claim when applied to intricate cases with many technicalities that required finesse in judgment. Despite the murkiness of the idea, fairness as a legal principle persisted through Roman law and into the early modern period.

What is the main idea?

How does the author or narrator feel about that?

"Plethora" Most Nearly Means

You've read the passage, continually asking yourself, "Self, what are the main idea and the tone?" Now, go to the questions. Unlike the questions in the math sections, the reading comprehension questions are not arranged in order of difficulty. Instead, they go in the order of the passage, with the main idea questions either first or last.

If the questions begin with the main idea, and you feel pretty sure about what that is, answer it. If you feel unsure about it, do the "line number" questions first. These are the ones that tell you what line number to look back at. Since we read quickly and did not obsess, we now have time to go back and reread the lines we need. By the time we've done all the line number questions, we will have reprocessed the passage and be even more sure of the main idea and the tone. This is an awesome strategy. This alone will raise your score.

When you answer a line number question, always go back and reread not only the line or lines that the question refers to, but also at least three lines before and after them. The answer usually comes before or after. If I say, "Vince Vaughn, the big man, is one facetious dude," I am probably expounding on what I said in the previous line or what I'm about to say in the next line. The next line would probably be: "Don't you agree, he's just the funniest guy," so now we know that "facetious" is related to "funny." That's how the SAT works. It always explains tough words nearby!

Let's take a look at the question from the Pretest.

3. In Passage 1 line 13, "will" most nearly means

(A) testament.   (B) stubbornness.   (C) being.   (D) desire.

Solution: This is a type of line number question. It always says, "Blah blah most nearly means." The answer to this type of question is rarely the obvious word that you'd pick if you hadn't even read the passage. It's usually one of the less obvious choices. To answer this question, go back to the line and reread a few lines before it and a few lines after it. In this case, the lines before contain the answer. "Now a strong believer in the power of the island, Locke knows that the place where they are stranded has a purpose for everyone. Following the **will** of the island . . . ." The word "will" as it is used here is related to "purpose," and the best answer is choice D.

Correct answer: D

SAT Reading/Writing Mantra #3
To answer a "most nearly means" question, reread a few lines before the question and a few lines after it, and remember that the answer is usually not the most common definition.

"Plethora" Most Nearly Means Drills

The following is adapted from a 2006 essay about poet Edna St. Vincent Millay. The author of the essay is referring to one of Millay's poems.

This is the energy that defines the flair and appeal of Edna St. Vincent Millay. She was always playing with fire, and at the same time shedding her lovely light for the world to admire. She was
5   lucky to be born in a time when people were ready to accept change, as Millay was always experimenting, and the world loved her for it. She was small in stature and had fiery red hair and a beautifully clear voice. The public adored
10   her charismatic, headstrong and passionate nature, and she fed their adoration with carefully crafted poems, articulating the thrill of her courageous and daring life.

She lived in Maine, by the sea, and her child-
15   hood was bleak. Her father left her mother when Edna was seven. They were incredibly poor, and her mother had to work hard to support the family. As a visiting nurse, young Millay's mother left her children alone a lot.
20   They were given chores, and it was up to Millay, the oldest, to inspire play from the work to keep the others happy. From this pinched childhood sprouted Millay's ability to dramatize and entertain.

1   In line 1, "flair" most nearly means

(A) signal.
(B) panache.
(C) flame.
(D) conflagration.

2   In line 9, the term "public" refers to

(A) all citizens.
(B) theater attendees.
(C) Millay's readers.
(D) a visiting nurse.

3   In line 11, "nature" most nearly means

(A) world.
(B) chronicle.
(C) environment.
(D) spirit.

4   In line 11, "adoration" most nearly means

(A) respect.
(B) desire.
(C) charisma.
(D) tenacity.

5   In line 15, "bleak" most nearly means

(A) austere.
(B) bland.
(C) weak.
(D) lonely.

6   "The others" in line 22 refers to

(A) Millay's public.
(B) Millay's parents.
(C) Millay's siblings.
(D) Millay's readers.

7   In line 22, "pinched" most nearly means

(A) twisted.
(B) wan.
(C) evil.
(D) virtuous.

Special Section: SAT Crashers
Rule #4: Process of Elimination

SAT Crashers Rule #4: Never cross out an answer choice unless you're **absolutely** positive of what it means and that it's wrong.

SAT Crashers Rule #5: No excuses. Test like a champion!

You probably never take multiple-choice tests in your English class at school. But the SAT is multiple choice, and you can use that to your advantage! After you have read a question and looked for evidence in the passage, cross out the answer choices that you are SURE do not fit. Cross out ONLY the choices that you are absolutely sure do not fit. This is very important; many people cross out options because they do not like them or do not understand them. Don't be crazy; cross out only the choices that definitely do not fit. Then, go through the remaining answer choices and choose the one that fits best.

> **SAT Reading/Writing Special Mantra**
> **Cross out answer choices that are definitely wrong.**
> **Then choose the best from what's left.**

Direct Info

"He's playing **fetch** . . . with my kids . . . he's treating my kids like they're dogs."
Debbie, *Knocked Up* (Universal Pictures, 2007)

This type of question asks you to retrieve info directly from the passage. No interpretation, no inferring, no thinking even. The key here is to be a dog; just play fetch. And be a lawyer. Read a little before and a little after the line number, and find **evidence** for an answer. Prove your answer with info from the passage.

Let's take a look at the question from the Pretest.

4. Passage 2 indicates that the principle to which Shepherd is most loyal is

   (A) leadership.
   (B) optimism.
   (C) chaos.
   (D) reason.

Solution: Always look for the evidence in the passage. Be a lawyer; find proof. This is true for all types of questions, but it's especially true for these direct info questions. All the answer choices for this question show up in the passage, but the passage states that Jack is a man who focuses on principles and fact and that he places a heavy emphasis on logic and reason. He does demonstrate leadership and optimism, and he is generally opposed to chaos (disorder), but according to the passage, he is **primarily** a man who is guided by reason.

Correct answer: D

SAT Reading/Writing Mantra #4
For a "direct info" question, always read before and after a line and find proof.

Direct Info Drills

The following passage is adapted from a scholarly paper that examines Yeats' poem "The Tower."

The Tower's three parts correspond to three stages of life, or three modes of relating to the world, but not in a scheme as simple as youth, adulthood and old age. Rather, the first and
5 third parts—or the first and third poems in a three-poem sequence—chart the internal experiences of an accelerating mind within a decelerating body. The second part is a more external reminiscence, passing elegiacally over the lore
10 of the land. The dying poet is taking a nostalgic survey of his works. The first and third parts take place within a dreaming mind, while the second takes place within the dream.

If we think of this poem as a ceremony, the first
15 part senses that the end is near, but is not ready to face it; the second part is a preparation ritual, and the third arrives at readiness and passes into nothing. If this passing is to have any meaning, the poet must propel himself enthu-
20 siastically into the next world rather than fall, withered and bedraggled, out of this one. To do so, he must find the memories in which he was most alive, maybe the ones that still hurt the most. These moments were truly his, and so are
25 truly his to leave behind.

1 In lines 1 and 2, "three stages of life" refers to

Ⓐ youth, adulthood, and old age.
Ⓑ baby, teenager, and adult.
Ⓒ the life cycle of a poem.
Ⓓ three ways of being in the world.

2 "The first and third poems" (lines 4 and 5) differ from the second in that

Ⓐ they are nostalgic.
Ⓑ they catalogue the poet's inner experience.
Ⓒ they are enthusiastic.
Ⓓ they are part of a cremation ceremony.

3 In lines 9 and 10, the phrase "passing elegiacally over the lore of the land" indicates that the poet was

Ⓐ a slow runner.
Ⓑ taking stock of his life's work.
Ⓒ working for the Census Bureau.
Ⓓ speaking at a funeral.

4 The author states that the poet must "find the memories . . . alive" (lines 22 and 23) in order to

Ⓐ leave this world with significance.
Ⓑ not die.
Ⓒ regain memories.
Ⓓ become alive.

5 The author compares the poem as a whole to

Ⓐ folklore.
Ⓑ a dying person.
Ⓒ a ceremony.
Ⓓ a memory.

rather = opinion

5

What Are You Trying to "Suggest"?

This type of question asks you what the author "suggests" or "implies," or what we can "infer." Whereas Skill 4 concerns questions that ask for information that's taken directly from the passage, like, "What color was Rosalie's convertible?" this question asks for information that was not given, but only hinted at, in the passage.

When students see this, they think that they have to use some crazy AP English logic. But, actually, the key is **not** to overthink the answer. For a "suggest" question, the correct answer will probably not be a direct quote from the passage, but it should be pretty darn close, and we must still have proof from the passage. The correct answer for any SAT question, even this type, should always be very close to what was directly stated in the passage.

> Here's the question from the Pretest.
>
> 5. The two passages suggest that a leader must do all of the following EXCEPT
>
>   (A) inspire followers.
>   (B) govern democratically.
>   (C) provide hope.
>   (D) have faith in others.

Solution: The word "suggest" tells us that the answer might not be directly stated. So do we freak out? Is the question too hard for us? No, sir; follow SAT Crashers Rule #16, "Don't look for problems; make answers!" Stay focused. Don't overthink it. The answer will be very close to something that's actually stated. Let's use the process of elimination.

(A) ~~inspire followers~~—Nope; both suggest that a leader must give "hope."
(B) govern democratically—Maybe, although only Passage 2 mentions it.
(C) ~~provide hope~~—No way; both directly suggest it.
(D) have faith in others—Maybe; do they both suggest it?

Choice B is the best answer because only Passage 2 discusses governing "democratically." Choice D is not correct because "faith in others" is stated directly in Passage 1 and suggested in Passage 2 with democratic leadership.

Correct answer: B

> **SAT Reading/Writing Mantra #5**
> For "suggest" questions, look for the answer that is hinted at in the passage;
> although it might use different language, it should be pretty close to
> what is actually said.

What Are You Trying to "Suggest"? Drills

Read the passage for the main idea and the tone, not to memorize details. We'll come back for those. Also, if you come to a crazy-hard sentence, don't reread it, move on. It's very liberating!

The following passage was included in a 1999 master's thesis about stress management.

The concept of biological stress refers to the body's response to any real or perceived threat to equilibrium. This stress response produces changes in the body in preparation for engag-
5 ing or running from a physical threat. These changes can include increased heart rate and blood pressure, muscle tension, and suspended digestive activity. In a physically threatening situation, this response is essential and can
10 be life-saving. However, after the threat has passed, the changes should abate and the body should return to normal.

The stress response can also be triggered by threats that are not solved by physical readi-
15 ness: traffic, work deadlines, or thinking of difficult future events. These threats are not solved by the stress response, and can persist for long periods or occur repeatedly. Thus, the stress response that is intended to turn on and then off
20 can become chronically activated. In this case, when the physiological changes of the stress response persist, the changes can lead to disease. Chronic stress has been linked to suppression of the immune system, rises in blood-cholesterol
25 levels, calcium loss from bones, long-term increases in blood pressure, increased muscle tension, diarrhea or digestive organ spasms, and risk of arrhythmia.

As a result of these potential problems, people
30 have explored ways of managing stress so it does not become chronic. The goal of stress management is not to avoid all stress, as some stress is inevitable and even stimulating, but to experience the stress response only when it is
35 relevant and helpful. Scientists studying stress and its management have found that stressors and stress management modalities affect individuals differently. A stressor that brings distress to one person may be pleasant for another.
40 Similarly, a stress management technique might work for one person, but be ineffective or even distressing for another.

1. The passage suggests that the "changes" described in lines 6–8 can be life-saving because they allow a person to

   Ⓐ tense up at the possibility of danger.
   Ⓑ avoid heart attack.
   Ⓒ deal with work deadlines.
   Ⓓ deal with material danger.

2. The reader can infer that the examples in lines 15 and 16 ("traffic . . . events.") are not solved by the stress response because

   Ⓐ they require physical readiness, not thinking.
   Ⓑ they persist too long.
   Ⓒ traffic and work deadlines are worsened by stress.
   Ⓓ the ability to fight or flee does not solve these concerns.

3. The last paragraph implies that stress management aims to

   Ⓐ avert the stress response when it cannot solve a problem.
   Ⓑ affect individuals differently.
   Ⓒ avoid all stress.
   Ⓓ raise one's heart rate.

Skill Preview:

4. (Skill 7) The author's attitude toward stress management is one of

   Ⓐ qualified disapproval.
   Ⓑ resentment.
   Ⓒ ambivalence.
   Ⓓ unbiased appreciation.

ASS of U and ME

Some questions will ask you to identify the assumptions that the author made in the passage. What's an SAT assumption? Here's an example. If I tell you that you must study to achieve your SAT goal, I have assumed that your goal is to do well on the SAT. We handle assumption questions as we do Skill 5's "suggest" questions: the correct answer will probably not be directly quoted from the passage, but it should be pretty darn close, and we must still have proof from the passage.

Let's take a look at the question from the Pretest.

6. In lines 13 to 16, the author of Passage 1 makes the assumption that

(A) the survivors want to start anew as John Locke did.
(B) John Locke was once paralyzed.
(C) John Locke feels no hope.
(D) Jack Shepherd was a successful surgeon.

Solution: Use the process of elimination, and remember to base your answer on evidence in the passage.

(A) the survivors want to start anew as John Locke did—Maybe; seems like an assumption.
(B) ~~John Locke was once paralyzed~~—No, this is fact.
(C) ~~John Locke feels no hope~~—No, there is no mention of this.
(D) ~~Jack Shepherd was a successful surgeon~~—No, that is Passage 2, and it is not an assumption anyway.

The answer has to be choice A. Even when a question seems weird or difficult, if you stay focused and use the process of elimination, you can get it right, sometimes without even being sure of the right answer!

Correct answer: A

SAT Reading/Writing Mantra #6
For an "assumption" question, use the process of elimination.

ASS of U and ME Drills

The following was adapted from an exploration of polarity, written in 2007.

Polarity is more complicated than many seem to understand. Indeed, I myself was surprised by the depths to which we may pursue any case of opposites. One astonishing example of this com-
5 plexity is that one opposite may, at an extreme, become the other. As a child in Waldorf kindergarten, I remember marveling with my friends at the water in which we washed the dishes from lunch, and how it was so hot that it felt
10 cold. We have all had the experience of laughing so hard that we cried, or feeling so happy that it hurt. In optics we see the color orange at the point where the top of a poorly lit window-frame meets the bright sky. At the bottom of the
15 window, where dark and light meet, we see its complementary color, blue.

Albert Einstein once stated that "Imagination is more important than knowledge." Einstein's fame as a scientist gives this quote tremendous
20 meaning. In one of the greatest minds of the modern world, one might expect a preference for knowledge over creativity, or hard work over play. Einstein, however, tells us not to discredit original thought, intuition, and the power
25 of our own minds.

Einstein also said, "Science without religion is lame, religion without science is blind." It is interesting to think that the two might go hand in hand, since we often think of science
30 and religion as being at war. Einstein obviously believed in the idea of these two polar opposites being complementary, rather than clashing.

Furthermore, to Einstein there exists a whole new level of religious understanding. "There
35 is a third stage of religious experience . . . even though it is rarely found in a pure form: I shall call it cosmic religious feeling." To Einstein, this is the level of pure religious feeling, separate from any taught concept of religion. It is man's
40 sense of right and wrong, his desire to do good and to help others.

---

1 In the first sentence, the author assumes that

  (A) no one can understand the true meaning of polarity.

  (B) people misunderstand polarity's implications.

  (C) others are not as intrigued as he is about polarity's depths.

  (D) one opposite may become another.

2 Lines 20–23 ("In one of the . . . play.") indicate that the author believes people might assume that Einstein

  (A) favored assiduous logical inquiry.

  (B) was pensive.

  (C) hated intellectualism.

  (D) favored religion over science.

3 A major assumption of the third paragraph is that

  (A) science and religion go hand in hand.

  (B) science and religion are considered opposites.

  (C) Einstein's experiments were invalid.

  (D) Einstein was devout.

Review

4 (Skill 3) In line 1, "polarity" most nearly means

  (A) complications.

  (B) magnetism.

  (C) apex.

  (D) opposites.

Special Section: The One Reading Comprehension Trick on the SAT

Reading comprehension questions are pretty straightforward. Your main task is to find the evidence for the answer. No deep analysis, leaps, or interpreting is needed. Once you really accept this, your score flies. There's really only one trick that the SAT attempts. Sometimes, in an answer choice, the first, let's say, six words will fit the evidence perfectly, but then the last one or two words will be way off. For example, if I am describing why you are reading this book, the answer might be "Hannah wants to improve the score on her ACT test." This is a perfect answer until the last two words. This book is for the SAT. Make sure to read the whole answer and check that the entire answer choice works, not just the first few words. Keep your eye out for this in the rest of the Reading Skills.

SAT Reading/Writing Special Section Mantra
Don't choose an answer unless all the words in your answer choice work. Don't be fooled by a choice in which the first part works and the last few words are wrong.

Vocabulary Special Section, Part I: Compliment or Insult?

The SAT tests vocabulary in context in Reading Comprehension questions. It doesn't really care whether you know the meaning of rare words like *perfidious* or *sycophantic*, which is good news, because, let's face it, you don't. But it does ask about more commonly used words like *satiated*, *ambivalent*, and *mediation*. The Vocabulary Special Sections on the next few pages will help you memorize or even figure out the meanings of words like these.

The first of these three strategies is called "Compliment or insult?" It works like this. If, for example, someone called you monochrome, would you feel happy or hurt? Think about it. *Monochrome* doesn't sound like a compliment; it actually sounds kinda negative. You don't want to be called monochrome. In fact, "monochrome" means "unvarying" or "dull and boring" and is definitely an insult, a negative word.

Here's another example. The word "lackluster" once showed up as an answer choice on an SAT. We needed a positive word as an answer choice, but tons of kids got to *lackluster* and said, "I don't know that word." Maybe they had never seen the word before, but there is no way that "lackluster" is a positive word. It has "lack" in it. In fact, it basically says, "lacking luster" or "without shine." And that's exactly what it means, "dull." So if you get a sense that a word is positive or negative, trust it. You can test a word by asking, "Would I want to be called that? Would I feel complimented or insulted?"

SAT Reading/Writing Special Section Mantra
If you're not sure of the meaning of a vocabulary word, ask yourself, "Would I want to be called that? Would I feel complimented or insulted?" That will give you a sense of whether the word is positive or negative.

Vocab I: Compliment or Insult Drills

Let's practice predicting whether words are positive, negative, or neither. You'll be surprised at how often you can tell, even when you think you don't know the word. Look at these vocab words and decide whether they are a compliment or an insult. Look at each word and ask, "Would I be psyched or insulted if Jenny called me _____?" Write +, –, or neither. Then check the solutions on page 195 to see if your feeling was correct.

a. peevish	j. flippant	s. dazzling
b. petulant	k. enthralling	t. resolute
c. sophisticated	l. vapid	u. pernicious
d. soporific	m. diminutive	v. disingenuous
e. saccharine	n. salutary	w. truculent
f. bombastic	o. magnanimous	x. diverting
g. magnificent	p. insipid	y. corrupt
h. abased	q. sagacious	z. charismatic
i. astute	r. baneful	

Vocabulary Special Section, Part II: Superbad Vocabulary

Some people say that to build your vocabulary, you must munch your toast with the *New York Times* and take Shakespeare to the beach. These are great suggestions that will certainly benefit you in many ways, but even without the *New York Times* and Shakespeare, you are already constantly surrounded by great vocabulary. So to build your vocab, you can also use what's already in front of you. Let's start with movies. Movies contain a ton of SAT vocab words.

Here' a great example from the movie *Juno* (Fox Searchlight Pictures, 2007):
<u>Juno</u>: No, this is not a food baby, all right? I've taken like three pregnancy tests, and I'm forshizz up the spout.
<u>Leah</u>: How did you even generate enough pee for three pregnancy tests? That's amazing. . . .
<u>Juno</u>: I don't know, I drank like, ten tons of Sunny D. Anyway dude, I'm telling you I'm pregnant and you're acting shockingly **cavalier**.

What did Juno mean by "cavalier"? You can get it from the words around it. Juno is telling Leah that she's pregnant, something that she is clearly upset about, and Leah doubts it and jokes around. Then Juno calls Leah "cavalier," so it must mean something like "too jokey" or "doubtful" or "not getting the seriousness here." And it does; "cavalier" means "too casual." Obviously, you may not memorize every new vocab word that comes at you while you are munching popcorn, but if you keep your ears open, you'll pick up some of them.

SAT Reading/Writing Special Section Mantra
Keep your ears open for vocabulary words. Just because you're watching the newest installment of the *Despicable Me* movie franchise doesn't mean that you can't be picking up new vocab words and upping your score!

Vocab II: Superbad Vocabulary Drills

Let's take a look at some of the most important cinematic moments of all time and the SAT vocab that we can learn from them. I'll give a quote from a movie, and you see if you can identify the movie and an approximate definition of the **bold** SAT vocabulary word.

1. Galadriel: . . . in the fires of Mount Doom, the Dark Lord Sauron forged in secret a master ring to control all others. And into this ring he poured all his cruelty, his **malice**, and his will to dominate all life.

   Movie _____

   "Malice" means _____

2. The Emperor: [*laughing*] Perhaps you refer to the **imminent** attack of your rebel fleet? Yes, I assure you, we are quite safe from your friends here.

   Movie _____

   "Imminent" means _____

3. Elizabeth: Captain Barbossa, I am here to **negotiate** the **cessation** of **hostilities** against Port Royal.

   Barbossa: There are a lot of long words in there, Miss; we're **naught** but **humble** pirates. What is it that you want?
   Elizabeth: I want you to leave and never come back.
   Barbossa: I'm **disinclined** to **acquiesce** to your request. Means "no."

   Movie _____

   "Negotiate" means _____

   "Cessation" means _____

   "Hostilities" means _____

   "Naught" means _____

   "Humble" means _____

   "Disinclined" means _____

   "Acquiesce" means _____

4. John Beckwith: [*about Chaz*] He lived with his mom til he was forty! She tried to poison his oatmeal!
   Jeremy Grey: **Erroneous**! **Erroneous**! **Erroneous** on both accounts!

   Movie _____

   "Erroneous" means _____

5. Soldier: Where'd you get the coconuts?
   King Arthur: We found them.
   Soldier: Found them? In Mercia? The coconut's tropical!
   King Arthur: What do you mean?
   Soldier: Well, this is a **temperate** zone.
   King Arthur: The swallow may fly south with the sun or the house martin or the plover may seek warmer climes in winter, yet these are not strangers to our land.

   Movie _____

   "Temperate" means _____

6. Murtogg: Someone's got to make sure that this dock stays off-limits to civilians.
   Jack Sparrow: It's a fine goal, to be sure. But it seems to me . . . that a ship like that one, makes this one here seem a bit **superfluous**, really.
   Murtogg: Oh, the *Dauntless* is the power in these waters, true enough. But there's no ship as can match the *Interceptor* for speed.
   Jack Sparrow: I've heard of one, supposed to be very fast, **nigh** uncatchable: *The Black Pearl*.

   Movie _____

   "Superfluous" means _____

   "Nigh" means _____

7. C-3PO: I am fluent in over six million forms of communication, and can readily . . .
   EV-9D9: Splendid! We have been without an interpreter since our master got angry with our last **protocol** droid and disintegrated him.

   Movie _____

   "Protocol" means _____

8 Ferris: I do have a test today. That wasn't bullshit. It's on European **socialism**. I mean, really, what's the point? I'm not European. I don't plan on being European. So who cares if they're socialists? They could be **fascist anarchists**. It still doesn't change the fact that I don't own a car. Not that I **condone** fascism, or any **-ism** for that matter.

Movie _____

"Socialism" means _____

"Fascist" means _____

"Anarchist" means _____

"Condone" means _____

"-ism" means _____

9 Albus Dumbledore: Cornelius, I **implore** you to see reason. The evidence that the Dark Lord has returned is **incontrovertible**.
 Cornelius Fudge: He is not back!

Movie _____

"Implore" means _____

"Incontrovertible" means _____

10 Virginia "Pepper" Potts: What do you want me to do with this?
Tony Stark: That? Destroy it. **Incinerate** it.
Virginia "Pepper" Potts: You don't want to keep it?
Tony Stark: Pepper, I've been called many things. **Nostalgic** is not one of them.

Movie _____

"Incinerate" means _____

"Nostalgic" means _____

This is a great way to learn and review vocabulary. Watch for vocab in your favorite movies and let me know what you notice at www.BrianLeaf.com. I'll include new quotes in future editions of this book.

Vocabulary Special Section, Part III: Deodorant and Spanish Class

When I was 17, the word "panache" was on my SAT. I didn't know the word, but I remembered that there was a fancy restaurant near my town called Café Panache. I thought, "What is panache?" Obviously this fancy restaurant was not called Café Smells Bad or Café I Hate You. (Some cafés might be called those names, but they would not be the places my parents would go.) So it had to be something like Café Delicious or Café Exciting or Café Good Times. That insight was enough to let me vibe the word and get the question right. In fact, "panache" is similar to "exciting"; it means "flair."

You can use anything around you to vibe out SAT vocab words. "Imperious" is an SAT word that stumps most kids. But you've definitely seen it or words like it around. You've heard of "Imperial Stormtroopers" or an "Imperial Cruiser" in *Star Wars* and the "Imperious Curse" in *Harry Potter*. From these references, you can certainly conclude that "imperious" must mean something like "big" or "grand" or "important," and that's enough to get an SAT question right. "Imperious" actually means "domineering, bossy, or authoritative." It makes sense that, in *Star Wars*, the Empire would have an Imperial Cruiser or that J. K. Rowling would use the word to describe a curse that gives someone control over another person!

So when you don't know a word or aren't sure of its definition, see if you can remember seeing or hearing the word or something like it anywhere—a billboard, a TV commercial, history class, Spanish class, *Harry Potter*, a restaurant name, a comic book, or *Magic: The Gathering* cards. Use anything that you can to figure it out.

SAT Reading/Writing Special Section Mantra
When you don't know a vocab word, see if you can remember seeing or hearing it or something like it anywhere—a billboard, a TV commercial, history class, Spanish class, *Harry Potter*, a restaurant name, a comic book, or *Magic: The Gathering* cards.

Vocab III: Deodorant and Spanish Class Drills

Here are some great SAT vocab words. Let's see if you can vibe them out. Even if you can't define them, try to come up with an association. That might be enough to tell you whether this word is the right or wrong answer on a sentence completion question. The goal here is not just for you to learn 13 new SAT words, but for you to become awake to all the great vocabulary that surrounds you.

Spanish

1 "Diverting" might mean _____.

2 "Facile" might mean _____.

French

3 "Luminance" might mean _____,

4 "Clairvoyant" might mean _____,

5 "Comportment" might mean _____,

6 "Filial" might mean _____,

The Grocery Store

7 "Arid" might mean _____.

Harry Potter

J. K. Rowling based the names of most charms and curses on English or Latin word parts. This is a font of SAT vocab; check out Wikipedia's entry for "Spells in Harry Potter."

8 "Impervious" might mean _____.

9 "Stupefy" might mean _____.

10 "Conflagration" might mean _____.

Dungeons & Dragons

All right, fess up and roll me a D20. D&D is a treasure chest of amazing SAT vocab words.

11 "Sagacious" might mean _____.

12 "Sylvan" might mean _____.

13 "Expeditious" might mean _____.

Vocabulary Special Section, Part IV: Splitting Words

Here's another great way to get a vibe for the meaning of a tough word. Many words in English break apart. For example, "anachronism" is a tough SAT word that most people don't know, but . . .

"A" or "an" means "not," like "amoral," "atypical," or "asymptomatic."

"Chron" means "time," like "chronological," "chronology," or "chronograph" (a stopwatch).

And "ism" doesn't change the meaning of a word much; it's just an ending that means "a practice or system."

Thus, "anachronism" means something like "a system not time." What? Confusing? Maybe, but it's enough to let you know whether the word applies or not. If you are looking for a word relating to time, it might be right; if you are looking for a word meaning "pertaining to trees," cross it out. In fact, "anachronism" means "something placed in the wrong time period," like Amelia wearing her digital watch while acting the role of Ophelia in Shakespeare's *Hamlet*.

SAT Reading/Writing Special Section Mantra
When you don't know a vocab word, see if you can break it apart.

Vocab IV: Splitting Words Drills

Use a dictionary to define the words in each group below, and then conclude what the word parts must mean.

① sympathy _____
apathy _____
pathetic _____

"path" means _____
"anti" means _____

empathy _____
pathos _____
antipathy _____

"a" means _____

② philanthropy _____
technophile _____
technology _____

"phil" means _____
"soph" means _____
"phobe" means _____

philosophy _____
technophobe _____
phobia _____

"anthro" means _____
"tech" means _____
"ology" means _____

③ terrestrial _____
extraterrestrial _____

"terr" means _____

terrain _____
extraordinary _____

"extra" means _____

④ homogeneous _____
homologous _____
homosexual _____

"homo" means _____
"gen" means _____

heterogeneous _____
heterologous _____
heterosexual _____

"hetero" means _____

⑤ circumscribe _____
circumvent _____
postscript _____
circumambulate _____
manuscript _____
transatlantic _____

"circum" means _____
"scribe" means _____
"re" means _____
"amb" means _____

circumnavigate _____
recirculate _____
transcribe _____
amble _____
manufacture _____

"post" means _____
"man" means _____
"trans" means _____

Here are a few more word parts. Can you define them?
"dis" means _____   "co" means _____   "sub" means _____

Some Attitude

Remember from Skill 2 that as you read each passage, you are keeping in mind, "What is the main idea and what is the author or narrator's attitude?" In this Skill, you will become an attitude master. An author's attitude is expressed through his or her choice of words and punctuation. For example, what is the attitude expressed in each of the following?

 Politicians have once again overlooked the need for improvement in the infrastructure.
Attitude toward politicians: disapproval

 Overworked politicians cannot be expected to foresee every need of their community.
Attitude toward politicians: compassion, forgiveness

③ Will Farrell is one funny guy.
Attitude toward Will Farrell: admiration, appreciation

④ You're such a "funny" guy.
Attitude: criticism, sarcasm

Remember to answer attitude questions based on evidence in the passage, not your own attitude toward the subject or any outside knowledge. If you need help, try rereading the first and last lines of each paragraph. Often, these lines convey the author's attitude.

The SAT favors mellow attitudes. An extreme answer with all-out hatred or complete, unqualified worship is usually not correct. The answer is generally more moderate. In fact, the correct answer often includes moderate words such as "moderate," "tempered," "qualified," "veiled," "relative," "somewhat," or "generally."

Let's take a look at the question from the Pretest.

7. The author of Passage 1 would most likely regard Dr. Jack Shepherd with

(A) absolute puzzlement.   (B) unabashed contempt.
(C) amusement.   (D) qualified disapproval.

Solution: Use the process of elimination. The author of Passage 2 describes John Locke as the **true** leader of the group and appreciates Locke's faith-based approach to leadership. She would therefore, at least to some extent, disagree with Jack's logic-based approach. We have no evidence that she would hate Jack, only that she appreciates Locke's style more. So we are looking for something neutral or slightly negative.

(A) ~~absolute puzzlement~~—Nope. The author does not seem puzzled, she seems sure.
(B) ~~unabashed contempt~~—Nope. The author never mentions hating Jack.
(C) ~~amusement~~—No, the author does not seem to be amused.
(D) qualified disapproval—Maybe; "qualified disapproval" means "limited disapproval."

Correct answer: D

SAT Reading/Writing Mantra #7
Answer "attitude" questions based on evidence in the passage; an author's attitude is expressed through his or her choice of words and punctuation.

Some Attitude Drills

The following is a monologue delivered in a 1998 movie. The speaker is about to scatter the ashes of his friend. (Courtesy of Universal Studios Licensing LLLP.)

Donny was a good bowler, and a good man. He was one of us. He was a man who loved the outdoors . . . and bowling, and as a surfer he explored the beaches of Southern California, from
5   La Jolla to Leo Carrillo and . . . up to . . . Pismo. He died, like so many young men of his genera-tion, he died before his time. In your wisdom, Lord, you took him, as you took so many bright, flowering young men at Khe Sanh, at Lang-
10   dok, at Hill 364.[1] These young men gave their lives. And so would Donny. Donny, who loved bowling. And so, Theodore Donald Karabotsos, in accordance with what we think your dying wishes might well have been, we commit your
15   final mortal remains to the bosom of the Pacific Ocean, which you loved so well. Good night, sweet prince.

1   In this passage, the speaker's attitude toward Donny is primarily one of

Ⓐ mournful eulogy.

Ⓑ unbiased detachment.

Ⓒ clear hostility.

Ⓓ elated nostalgia.

2   The speaker's attitude toward bowling can best be described as

Ⓐ respect.

Ⓑ disregard.

Ⓒ contempt.

Ⓓ indifference.

3   In context, the tone of lines 7 to 10 ("In your wisdom . . . Hill 364.") is best described as

Ⓐ anxious.

Ⓑ impatient.

Ⓒ baffled.

Ⓓ resigned.

4   The speaker's tone in the last two sentences is best described as

Ⓐ irritated.

Ⓑ confused.

Ⓒ solemn.

Ⓓ encouraged.

Review

5   (Skill 3) In line 8, "bright" most nearly means

Ⓐ light.

Ⓑ intelligent.

Ⓒ vivid.

Ⓓ dazzling.

6   (Skill 3) In context, "bosom" (line 15) most nearly means

Ⓐ chest.

Ⓑ column.

Ⓒ trunk.

Ⓓ comfort.

7   (Skill 5) The reference to Khe Sanh and Langdok in lines 9 and 10 suggests that

Ⓐ Donny will be buried at Hill 364.

Ⓑ Donny died in combat.

Ⓒ the speaker misses these places.

Ⓓ the speaker also lost friends at these places.

[1]Battles of the Vietnam war.

Every SAT includes at least one pair of passages and asks you to compare and contrast them. There is a superb strategy for dealing with these:

SAT Reading/Writing Mantra #8
When there are two passages, read the first passage for the main idea and the tone and answer any questions that ask about Passage 1. Then read the second passage for the main idea and the tone and answer questions about that passage. Finally, answer questions that compare and contrast the two passages.

The questions usually contain trick answers from the other passage, but if you haven't even read it, then you can't be fooled by the tricks. They'll just seem irrelevant, and you'll eliminate those choices immediately.

After you read Passage 1, jot down or circle a phrase that identifies the main idea or the tone. Then, after you answer the Passage 1 questions, read Passage 2 for the main idea and the tone, and jot down or circle a phrase. This will help you keep the passages straight for the compare and contrast questions.

Also, generally, if the passages are about the same topic, they will have a slightly different take on it. And if they are about different topics, then they will share a common link uniting them. For example, if both passages are about MP3 players, they will have slightly different opinions or focus on different aspects of the topic, such as the benefits of portability versus the reduction in sound quality. And if they are on totally different topics, such as Shakespeare and Eminem, they will have something in common, such as praising the extraordinary poetry of each.

Let's look at the question from the Pretest.

8. The author of Passage 2 would most likely regard John Locke with

(A) reverence.
(B) indifference.
(C) skepticism.
(D) caustic abhorrence.

Solution: The author of Passage 2 respects Jack's logical nature and compliments Jack on avoiding "hokey mysticism." She would therefore disapprove of John Locke's faith-based approach to leadership on the island. Therefore, choice C is a possible answer. The author does not abhor (hate) Locke; she just thinks that Jack is the better leader.

Remember, an extreme answer with all-out hatred or complete, unqualified worship is not usually correct. Usually the answer is more moderate.

Correct answer: C

Two Passages Drills

Passage 1

Medicinal systems can be examined by using
three models: biochemical, bioenergetic, and
biospiritual. The biochemical model is the dominant approach used in the United States. Scien-
5　tists using this approach analyze the chemical
constituents of things. It views the human body
as a chemical factory that can be adjusted according to the intake of the right chemicals. This
model tends to employ medicinal drugs, called
10　pharmaceuticals. These drugs are made by
identifying therapeutic substances and isolating
their active ingredients. These drugs often have
a stronger potency and a more immediate effect
on the body than nonisolated and natural rem-
15　edies, but often, later, it is found that they have
unanticipated side effects or that the pathogenic
factors change, rendering the drug less effective.

Passage 2

Ayurveda is a 5000-year-old natural healing
system from India. The word "Ayurveda" trans-
20　lates from Sanskrit as "the science of life or lon-
gevity." It can be described as a natural holistic
medical system. Dr. Andrew Weil describes
natural medical systems as having a philosophy
of healing based on the notion that the body has
25　innate mechanisms of self-repair—for example,
that a cut on the human body will naturally
heal itself. The aim in Ayurveda is to observe
and then encourage the self-repair process: to
empower the body's natural healing potential.
30　Ayurveda is also a type of holistic medicine, as
it considers the effect of a whole substance on
the whole of a person, rather than only a body
part or system.

1　In Passage 1, the author cites which of the
following as an example of a biochemical
medicine?

Ⓐ Nonisolated remedies

Ⓑ Pharmaceuticals

Ⓒ Holistic medicine

Ⓓ Natural remedies

2　The author of Passage 2 makes use of all of the
following except

Ⓐ generalizations.

Ⓑ refuting a hypothesis.

Ⓒ defining a term.

Ⓓ citing an authority.

3　The author of Passage 1 would most likely
regard the system of Ayurveda as described in
lines 30–33 ("Ayurveda . . . system.") in
Passage 2 as

Ⓐ a biochemical system.

Ⓑ inactive.

Ⓒ either bioenergetic or biospiritual.

Ⓓ inferior to the dominant approach.

4　Both passages serve to encourage

Ⓐ the body's self-repair.

Ⓑ consideration of the whole effect of medicines on the body.

Ⓒ the need for medical reform.

Ⓓ the lack of continuity in medical systems.

5　A primary difference between the two
passages is

Ⓐ the first begins to set up a basis for analyzing any medical system, whereas the second
begins to detail one specific system.

Ⓑ the first is specific and the second is general.

Ⓒ the first encourages holistic health and the
second discourages it.

Ⓓ the first discusses one system and the second discusses several.

Main Idea

The main idea is the general topic of a passage, what it's trying to get across. It answers the question, "So, what's your point?" That's the question that you kept in mind as you read the passage. Reading with this question in mind helps you

- Stay focused
- Avoid getting caught up in memorizing details
- Gather an answer for the "main idea" question

After you have answered all the line number questions, go back to the main idea and tone questions. Why wait? Because by the time you have completed the line number questions, you have reread and rethought the passage and you have an even better understanding of the main idea and the tone.

Also, remember the intro paragraph. I showed you in Skill 1 that the intro sometimes actually gives away the main idea! If you need more help, you can also reread the first and last lines of each paragraph for clues to the main idea.

Here's the question from the Pretest.

9. The passage is best described as

(A) an illustration of an ongoing relationship.
(B) an introduction to a character.
(C) a social commentary on the Western genre.
(D) a nostalgic depiction of a Western hero.

Solution: Think of a basic answer that you would like to see and then use the process of elimination. Don't get thrown by a wrong answer that sounds fancy. Stay confident. Kids sometimes think, "Wow, that sounds fancy. I don't get it, but it must be right." No! The right answer should make sense to you. It should fit the evidence in the passage. Be a lawyer! Let's take a look:

(A) an illustration of an ongoing relationship—Maybe, but this is kinda weak/ It is not really about an ongoing relationship.
(B) an introduction to a character—Maybe, but this is also weak. It seems more about Westerns in general than about any specific character.
(C) a social commentary on the Western genre—Probably. It is certainly mostly about Westerns in general.
(D) ~~a nostalgic depiction of a Western hero~~—No, it's not the story of a particular hero.

Choice C is the best answer. The passage is primarily about Westerns and the changes in their style over the years. You can see this very clearly by rereading the first and last lines of each paragraph!

Correct answer: C

SAT Reading/Writing Mantra #9
**If you need help with a "main idea" question, reread the intro
paragraph and the first and last lines of each paragraph.**

Main Idea Drills

Olmsted foresaw the need for plans at a time when they were considered mysterious. He anticipated that city parks would ensure future prosperity for the cities by increasing the value of city real estate, as well as creating a more balanced and egalitarian life for city dwellers then and in the future. Olmsted possessed an ability to see into the future and address the future needs of city dwellers in his planning. In this way, his planning had a permanent effect on history that remains pertinent to our modern lifestyles. Even today, his concepts of city parks and landscaping are widely accepted and practiced.

1. The author's main point in the passage is that

   (A) city parks are essential to city real estate.

   (B) Olmsted was a man of vision.

   (C) city park planning has not changed much since Olmsted's time.

   (D) Olmsted sought egalitarian city park use.

During the tower's construction, many Parisian citizens complained about the tower's aesthetics, inconvenience, and potential danger. Some people went so far as to testify in court. A number of well-known artists and musicians got together to sign a petition against the tower. They stated that it was ugly, useless, costly, and likely to fall in harsh weather. Gustave replied to the complaints by saying that he was as dedicated to the tower's aesthetics as they were, and that he designed the tower in such a way that the iron lattice work created almost no wind resistance, thus ensuring the tower's endurance.

2. The primary purpose of the passage is to

   (A) depict an era.

   (B) justify an expenditure.

   (C) give an historical account.

   (D) defend a decision.

Ma makes sassafras tea while Pa's boss compliments the tree. Then, they all sit down for grown-up talk while we gather round the tree to shake the copious presents. When carolers come by, we witness the enchanted looks on their faces as they too are inebriated by the magic of the gorgeous tree. Then Ma gives them some gingerbread and cider. If we had a tree like this, we'd never travel to Brooklyn to see Grandma; she'd come to us, despite the fact that she hates our dogs.

3. The passage is best described as

   (A) an illustration of a lasting relationship.

   (B) a nostalgic recollection.

   (C) a pleasant fantasy.

   (D) a story of imminent change.

Best Evidence

Many students complain that "best evidence" questions are unfair: "If you get the first one wrong, you have to get the second one wrong, too!" I also thought this at first. But, it turns out that these questions are actually even easier than other question types once you know how to approach them. Here's the strategy: Answer the "best evidence" question first then go back and answer the previous question. For the "best evidence" question, read the four answer choice options and decide which one actually answers the previous question. That's your answer, AND it gives you the evidence for the previous question.

> Let's see this on the pretest.
>
> **10.** Which choice provides the best evidence for the answer to the previous question?
>
>   (A) lines 1–2 ("The … years")
>   (B) lines 10–17 ("From … same")
>   (C) lines 18–19 ("A … change")
>   (D) lines 23–28 ("In … Beautiful")

Solution: These questions are a great opportunity to get two questions correct. Read each answer choice to determine which lines answer the previous question, "The passage is best described as". All of the answer choices are excerpts from the passage, and all of them are relevant to the themes in the work, but only one answers the previous question, to describe the *main idea* of the passage. Answer choice B, "From one to the other, the myth of pure masculinity has become convoluted, the male hero less omnipotent, the not always moral White settler less a symbol of 'Family Values,' and America less of a pristine, idealized dream" best captures not just a single theme of the passage, but the main idea. And now we know the answer to the previous question as well: the passage is "a social commentary on the Western genre." And remember to use the process of elimination.

Correct answer: B

Reading/Writing Mantra # 10
For "best evidence" questions, read the four options and decide which one actually answers the previous question. That's your answer, AND it gives you the evidence you need for the previous question as well.

Best Evidence Drills

This passage is from a 2015 book that explores certain health trends.

Science is telling us that too much sugar isn't good for anyone. A study in the *British Journal of Psychiatry* of more than 3000 participants found that those who had a diet high in sugar had a
5 58 percent increased risk for depression. Interestingly, those whose diet, instead, contained more whole foods, like veggies, fruits, and fish, had a 26 percent reduced risk for depression. Similarly, research presented at the American
10 Academy of Neurology's annual meeting in 2013 showed that people who drank more than four cups per day of soda were 30 percent more likely to develop depression. And long-term, a study of 30,000 individuals over 25 years
15 determined that people who get more than 15 percent of their total daily calories from sugar have a substantially increased risk of dying of heart disease.

According to the U.S. Department of Agri-
20 culture the average American consumes 156 pounds of added sugar per year. That's almost half a pound per day. Between the sodas and muffins and ice cream, you've got forty-eight teaspoons of added sugar per day. That's a tea-
25 spoon every twenty minutes all day that you're awake. It's no surprise that we are one of the most depressed countries. Often ranked number one, in fact.

Why do we eat so much sugar? Neuroscience
30 explains it this way. In order for us to survive as a species, activities such as eating and nurturing offspring must be pleasurable. This encourages and reinforces the behavior, so we repeat it. When we eat something yummy, an area of the
35 brain called the ventral tegmental releases the neurotransmitter dopamine which signals the prefrontal cortex, a part of the brain that helps us decide whether or not to take another bite of that delicious chocolate cake. So dopamine
40 ensures we continue eating yummy things and telling our kids to tie their shoelaces.

Current thinking in neuroscience suggests that, evolutionarily, this "natural reward" loop for food primarily reinforces sweet tastes. When Og
45 was scavenging for berries, a sour taste meant "not yet ripe," while a bitter flavor indicated "Stop! Potential poison!?" But a sweet taste said, "Hey, here is some readily digestible carbs for good clean energy!"

50 All of this was absolutely terrific for Og and his cousin Zog. Their ventral-tegmental-prefrontal-cortex loop kept them high on berries and caring for their young. Humanity thrived. Until recently, with the advent of the brownie that beat
55 the system and messed everything up. Now, our neurotransmitters are lying to us. Worse, we've become hooked on these processed sugars. Increasing evidence suggests that sugar, like nicotine, cocaine, and heroin, hijacks the natu-
60 ral reward pathway, making users dependent. Regular sugar consumption leads to prolonged dopamine signaling, causing increased tolerance and the need for more sugar to activate the natural reward high. Conversely, that's why, if
65 you give up sugar for a few weeks, suddenly an apple tastes as sweet and delicious as a brownie and an actual brownie tastes way too sweet.

1 The author indicates that sugar is addictive because

(A) humans care more for their young than for their own survival.

(B) sugar is found in great concentration in wild berries.

(C) humans are meant to eat only meats and vegetables.

(D) eating a lot of sugar causes the need for an increased amount of sugar before the dopamine reaction is triggered.

2 Which choice provides the best evidence for the answer to the previous question?

(A) Lines 1–5 (Science . . . depression.)

(B) Lines 30–32 (In order . . . must be pleasurable)

(C) Lines 61–64 (Regular sugar consumption . . . natural reward high)

(D) Lines 44–49 (When Og was scavenging . . . good clean energy!)

3 The author indicates that Og and Zog ate sweet foods because

  Ⓐ they were not yet able to use fire to cook meat.

  Ⓑ the sweet taste told them that the foods were safe to eat.

  Ⓒ other, more complex foods were not yet available.

  Ⓓ this was the recommendation of neuroscientists.

4 Which choice provides the best evidence for the answer to the previous question?

  Ⓐ Lines 13–18 (And long-term, . . . dying of heart disease.)

  Ⓑ Lines 47–49 (But a sweet taste . . . clean energy!)

  Ⓒ Lines 61–64 (Regular sugar consumption . . . the natural reward high)

  Ⓓ Lines 29–32 (Neuroscience explains it . . . must be pleasurable)

Table

Certain questions ask you about a table or graph that is shown at the end of the passage. Treat these exactly like Direct Info questions. Find the evidence, then use a process of elimination to choose the best answer. Most important, don't be intimidated. There won't be any fancy math here. You won't need to do calculations. Don't look for a trick. Look for a straightforward answer that has clear and easy evidence right in the graph. I'm not kidding, and I'm not oversimplifying this. It's easier than you think; your mission here is to look for the easy answer. This one change, from thinking of these as tricky to realizing that they are easy and very straightforward, usually helps my students get every table/graph question correct.

Here's the question from the pretest:

11. Based on the table and the passage, which film best captures the Western genre?

(A) *Stagecoach*
(B) *Dead Man*
(C) *True Grit*
(D) The passage and the table do not indicate which film best captures the Western genre.

Solution: Don't be intimidated or tricked. Neither the passage nor the table indicates anything about one film best capturing the genre. The SAT will give you clear and obvious evidence for the answer to a reading comprehension question. Don't overthink it or look for tricks. If your answer requires leaps of logic that are not mentioned in the passage, then it's not the correct SAT answer. For example, you might think, "*True Grit* has the highest revenue, so it must best capture the genre," but we don't really know that to be true. Maybe it's a terrible example of the genre. We just don't know from the evidence. If the SAT wants to say that one film is the best example, it will clearly state that. The right answer will have clear and straightforward evidence in the passage.

Correct answer: D

> **SAT Reading/Writing Mantra #11**
> **Don't get intimidated by questions that refer to a table or graph. Treat them like any other question—find the evidence and use the process of elimination.**

Table Drills

For the following questions, refer to the passage in the Skill 10 Drills on page 51.

The table below shows, for various foods, the total sugar and calorie content in an 85-gram serving.

	Apple	Grapes	Brownie
Total sugar (g)	8.8	13.2	42
Calories	44	57	396
Fat (g)	0.3	0.34	24

1 Do the data in the table support the authors' proposed explanation of why sugar is now more prevalent in food than it was thousands of years ago?

Ⓐ No, because for each food listed, the number of calories varies by a factor that is inconsistent with standard scientific methods.

Ⓑ No, because for the foods listed, the grams of sugar in a brownie far exceed the grams of sugar in a serving of either apple or grapes, which is inconsistent with the author's main argument.

Ⓒ Yes, because for each food listed, the number of calories increases.

Ⓓ Yes, because for the foods listed, the sugar content in the brownie far exceeds the sugar content in either the apple or the grapes, which is consistent with the author's argument.

2 According to the table, which of the following amounts of sugar in grams in common foods provides evidence in support of the answer to the previous question?

Ⓐ 8.8 and 44

Ⓑ 13.2 and 57

Ⓒ 8.8, 13.2, and 42

Ⓓ 44, 57, and 396

3 Based on the table, which food has the lowest sugar to calorie ratio?

Ⓐ Apples

Ⓑ Grapes

Ⓒ Brownies

Ⓓ Cannot be determined from the information given

4 Based on the table and the passage, which foods would the authors assert were most like the kinds of food regularly consumed by Og and Zog?

Ⓐ Apples

Ⓑ Brownies

Ⓒ Apples and grapes

Ⓓ Grapes and brownies

Gretchen Is "Such" a Good Friend

And you know she cheats on Aaron? Yes, every Thursday he thinks she's doing SAT prep, but really she's hooking up with Shane Oman in the projection room above the auditorium! I never told anybody that because I am "such" a good friend!

Gretchen, *Mean Girls* (Paramount Pictures, 2004)

Why are there quote marks around "such"? In this example, it's to show that the word is emphasized. The SAT loves to ask questions like this, questions about why the author chose a certain word, punctuation mark, or phrase. These questions ask about the writer's choices and how a word functions, rather than about the main idea or what a word means.

Let's look at the question from the Pretest.

12. In line 13, the quotation marks around the words "Family Values" serve to

(A) criticize the Western genre.
(B) indicate an irony in the meaning of the words.
(C) emphasize the uniqueness of the author's writing.
(D) support the common use of the words.

Solution: Usually, on the SAT, when quotation marks are not used literally to quote something, they indicate that the word or phrase is being used in an unusual way, such as ironically. In this case, the settler is described as "not always moral," so "Family Values" is being used ironically. You could convince yourself of several of the other answers, but choice B is the best answer and the one that is most clearly supported by evidence in the passage. Remember to base your answer on evidence in the passage, not your own outside knowledge or opinions.

Correct answer: B

> **SAT Reading/Writing Mantra #12**
> When quotes around a phrase are not used to literally quote something from another source, they indicate that the phrase is being used in an unusual way, such as ironically. And words in parentheses usually function as a side note to the reader.

Gretchen Is "Such" a Good Friend Drills

This passage is from a 1998 movie. (Courtesy of Universal Studios Licensing LLLP.)

Way out west there was this fella I wanna tell
ya about. Goes by the name of Jeff Lebowski.
At least that was the handle his loving parents
gave him, but he never had much use for it
5   himself. See, this Lebowski, he called himself
"The Dude." Now, "Dude"'s a name no man
would self-apply where I come from. But then
there was a lot about the Dude that didn't make
a whole lot of sense. And a lot about where he
10 lived, likewise. But then again, maybe that's
why I found the place so darned interestin'. See,
they call Los Angeles the "City of Angels"; but
I didn't find it to be that, exactly. But I'll allow
it as there are some nice folks there. 'Course I
15 ain't never been to London, and I ain't never
seen France. And I ain't never seen no queen in
her damned undies, so the feller says. But I'll
tell you what—after seeing Los Angeles, and
this here story I'm about to unfold, well, I guess
20 I seen somethin' every bit as stupefyin' as you'd
seen in any of them other places. And in English, too. So I can die with a smile on my face,
without feelin' like the good Lord gypped me.

Now this here story I'm about to unfold took
25 place in the early '90s—just about the time of
our conflict with Sad'm and the I-raqis. I only
mention it because sometimes there's a
man . . . I won't say a hero, 'cause, what's a hero?
Sometimes, there's a man. And I'm talkin' about
30 the Dude here—the Dude from Los Angeles.
Sometimes, there's a man, well, he's the man for
his time and place. He fits right in there. And
that's the Dude. The Dude, from Los Angeles.
And even if he's a lazy man—and the Dude was
35 most certainly that. Quite possibly the laziest in
all of Los Angeles County, which would place
him high in the runnin' for laziest worldwide.
Sometimes there's a man, sometimes, there's a
man. Well, I lost my train of thought here.
40 But . . . aw, hell. I've done introduced it enough.

---

1 The author misspells words in lines 1 and 2
("Way out . . . about") in order to

  Ⓐ represent the narrator's accent.

  Ⓑ indicate his disapproval of the accepted
spellings.

  Ⓒ emphasize the uniqueness of the author's
writing.

  Ⓓ criticize the character being described.

2 In line 6, the quotation marks around the word
"The Dude" serve to

  Ⓐ emphasize the individuality of the author's
style.

  Ⓑ indicate the unusualness of the name.

  Ⓒ indicate the narrator's disapproval of
Lebowski.

  Ⓓ criticize Lebowski's parents.

3 The repetition of the phrase "sometimes there's
a man" in lines 27 to 29 emphasizes the

  Ⓐ narrator losing concentration.

  Ⓑ infrequent appearances of the Dude.

  Ⓒ doubt as to the Dude's gender.

  Ⓓ Dude's laziness.

4 The author develops the passage by presenting

  Ⓐ a hypothesis and supporting details.

  Ⓑ a common argument followed by counterexamples to disprove it.

  Ⓒ a description interspersed with tangential
remarks.

  Ⓓ several sides to a single issue.

Review

5 (Skill 3) In line 3, "handle" most nearly means

- (A) grip.
- (B) inheritance.
- (C) ability to cope.
- (D) title.

6 (Skill 2) The phrase "but I didn't . . . exactly" (line 12) indicates that the narrator

- (A) could not locate the city.
- (B) did not attend church in Los Angeles.
- (C) met few virtuous people in Los Angeles.
- (D) met several nice people in the city.

Parallel

This question type asks, Which of the following ideas or situations is most like (or unlike) the one from the passage? This type of question throws students because the choices are not details from the passage. They are new details that exemplify something from the passage, and we want the one that satisfies the question.

Kids get confused by these and say, "Oh, I don't recognize these choices. I must have missed this; I'll just skip this one." But with our strategies, you won't miss anything. Stay relaxed and focused and confident. And when you see this type of question, just recognize it as a "parallel" question and know that the choices may not be from the passage. Since you're expecting it, you'll recognize it and get it right.

Let's take a look at the Pretest.

13. Which statement about Westerns, if true, detracts most from the author's assertions expressed in lines 15 to 18 ("both films . . . same")?

(A) Both films have a similar style.
(B) Both films examine the theme of love and loss.
(C) *Dead Man* and *Stagecoach* each stick to predictable Western patterns.
(D) *Dead Man* and *Stagecoach* examine different subject matter.

Solution: The author's assertions say that even though there are big differences, there are also **similarities** in style and theme. To detract most from this, you want an answer that says the opposite—that points out the style and/or theme **differences** between the two films. Choice D is the only choice that points out differences. On this type of question, make sure to stay confident, and as you look through the choices, remember whether you want differences or similarities.

Correct answer: D

SAT Reading/Writing Mantra #13
For a "parallel" question, don't get thrown if the choices are not from the passage.
Stay relaxed and focused, and look for the choice that proves
or disproves the statement.

Parallel Drills

The media makes you think that you have to be skinny or buff. The media makes you think that you have to get rich and own lots of things. But you don't. I see a whole generation; no, I see
5 generations working as slaves to consumption. Working, working too hard to buy disposable things they're told they need. Go sit by a tree in a calm place for two hours, maybe by a stream. You'll see what I mean. It's free and it's more
10 joy than that new designer watch can possibly give you.

Why is everyone depressed? Their latte is not making them happy. Two-and-a-half hours of TV per day is not satisfying. People are
15 confused by TV; their expectations of life get skewed. No, there's a void. Relax, open, and let it fill up.

1 Which of the following individuals best exemplifies the narrator's assertion in lines 1 to 3 ("The media . . . things.")?

Ⓐ A man who saves up to buy a new designer suit

Ⓑ A man who hates his job and quits

Ⓒ A man who finds a job that he loves

Ⓓ A slave in chains

2 Which of the following is the narrator likely to do next?

Ⓐ Teach more about designer watches

Ⓑ Give Latin names for specific trees

Ⓒ Describe more about how individuals can take action to effect change

Ⓓ Describe jobs that are available

3 Which of the following, if true, would LEAST undermine the assertion in lines 13 to 16 ("Two and . . . skewed.")?

Ⓐ Most people do not try to model what they see on television.

Ⓑ Most people do not realize that what they see on television is unreal.

Ⓒ Most people watch far less than 2.5 hours of television per day.

Ⓓ A study showed that most people are very minimally affected by the values expressed on television.

Review

4 (Skill 9) The general tone of the passage can best be described as

Ⓐ humorous contempt.

Ⓑ worried vexation.

Ⓒ relieved acknowledgment.

Ⓓ muted anger.

Special Section: How to Read

Sometimes SAT passages are obscenely long and kids panic, "I can't do it! It'll take too long. It'll kill me." Relax, and remember your skills. Read the passage, looking for the main idea and the tone. Don't memorize details. Don't reread a confusing line. Don't reread if you spaced out and missed a sentence or two. There's no single sentence or even paragraph that you need in order to get the main idea and the tone. As for details, you'll reread the lines later anyway.

All this will save you time and energy. And remember my story. When I was 16 years old and preparing for the SAT, I did well in school, but I didn't read much. I was terrified. Then one day I was like, "Wait, this is ridiculous; how long can it take?" So I took out a stopwatch and timed myself. It took 2.5 minutes! Try it, and you'll see. Even for a slow reader, the passage takes only a few minutes, especially if you use your skills.

So read the following huge passage. Read quickly, but stay relaxed. Pretend that you love the topic. As you read, ask yourself, What are the main idea and the tone? Use all the Skills. Time yourself. You'll see that reading even a ridiculously long passage takes only a few minutes.

> **How to Read**
> - **Read the passage, looking for the main idea and the tone.**
> - **Don't memorize details.**
> - **Don't reread a confusing line.**
> - **Don't reread if you spaced out and missed a sentence or two.**

Directions: Read the absurdly long passage on the next page. Time yourself. If it takes you more than 5 minutes, review the Skills above and reread the passage. Anyone can read quickly; remember, you are not reading to memorize details, just to get the gist. You'll see that reading even a disgustingly long SAT passage takes only a few minutes. When it takes you less than 5 minutes, you're ready.

(If you absolutely cannot do it in under 5 minutes, no problem. Here's your strategy: read for 4 minutes and stop. That'll be enough for you to get some main idea and tone info without spending too much time. But you have to practice watching the clock and knowing when it's been 4 minutes.)

This passage describing a certain type of spider was written in 2006.

The Brown Recluse spider is a potentially dangerous species that inhabits the southeastern part of the United States. A bite from the Brown Recluse can cause a severe wound. As a result, the spiders cause much fear; however, in reality, Brown Recluse spiders cause few grave injuries to humans, and you are more likely to get struck by lightning than critically hurt by a Brown Recluse spider.

Including its legs, the Recluse spider is roughly the size of a quarter. Females have a slightly larger body than the males; however, the males make up for this with longer legs—better for hunting. The only way for an everyday person (not a trained scientist) to identify this spider is the darker brown fiddle-shaped marking on the back of the abdomen. This is how they acquired their nickname Fiddler Spider.

The Recluse spider lives about two years, taking about a year to fully mature, molting clear bridal exoskeletons several times on their way to adulthood. The females lay their eggs in white silky sacks, each containing roughly forty spider-larva. A female can lay several sacks a season, sometimes even producing up to 300 individual eggs. The mother remains in her web to guard the eggs until the spiderlings emerge. During this period of twenty to thirty days, the mother doesn't eat or drink, not letting her attention waver at all from her offspring.

The spiderlings abandon the web immediately after they hatch; they leave to find their secluded hideaways and to give their mother back her preferred solitary life. The young spiders enter the world as immature lentil-sized versions of their parents. Their only major defense is their freakish ability to fast for up to six months without food or water—their poison hasn't even peaked in its potency. Most of them will die on their eleven-month journey to adulthood. Come next year the small handful of time-tested troopers will be mature in time to take part in breeding season. This is most likely their first of two breedings.

The Brown Recluse spider uses its web as a private day lodging. They do not use it as a hunting palate like most spiders do. Their web is also unusual in that it doesn't have a pleasing symmetrical spiral pattern of tightly woven clean threads. On the contrary it is rough, lacking order, comprised of loose strands of off-yellow silk sagging in all directions. The web seems to be of little use to these spiders and the project of building can even be abandoned if a soft nesting place, such as stored linens or clothes, is available.

The spiders tend to leave their lone retreats at sundown to hunt for insects. They kill their prey by initially using their legs to trap the insect and then injecting their venom to finish the job. Although they can hunt and have evolved venom to do so, their weak physical constitution renders hunting second to scavenging. Their legs fall off easily, and if a spider is not quick enough to inject the venom, it is possible for the prey to shred it to pieces. This often happens with crickets. Changing habitats have also fostered their growing love of dead insects. With more and more Recluses living in human environments, dried out bugs are all around them and easily picked up during the night when the inhabitants are sleeping.

The spiders tend to spin their webs in dark reclusive sheltered areas, and consequently man-made buildings meet their needs perfectly. They can be invasive pests, monopolizing attics, barns, cellars, and crawl spaces with their ugly webs. Their need for private spaces quickly disperses a colony throughout a building.

In North America the Brown Recluse spider ranks with the rattlesnake, black widow, cougar, and grizzly in its threat to people. Yet, problematic injuries actually rarely happen. In fact, you are more likely to croak in your bathtub than from a bite from a Brown Recluse spider. However, I don't buy it, I'm the first to avoid grizzly bear territory, and next time I go South, I plan on sleeping in a body bag with microscopic breathing holes.

How to Be a Reading Ninja

You've now learned the 13 reading Skills that you need for the SAT. The Mantras remind you of what to do for each type of question. Let's make sure you've memorized them. Drill them until you are ready to teach them. Then do that. Find a willing friend and give a little SAT course.

Learning the Mantras is like learning martial arts. Practice until they become part of you—until you can follow them naturally: When you see a passage, you read for the main idea and the tone, and when you answer questions, you recognize most question types and know what to do with each. This will definitely raise your score. It might even fundamentally change you as a student. After SAT prep, many students have better study habits. They read the intros in their history book; they read faster and with better comprehension; they are able to anticipate quiz questions. Homework becomes less intimidating, easier, and more fun. So go to work—your SAT score and probably your school grades as well will go up!

Here are the 13 SAT reading Mantras. Check the box next to each Skill when you have mastered it. Reread the Skill sections if you need to.

☐ **Skill 1.** Always begin a reading passage by reading the intro paragraph.

☐ **Skill 2.** Read the passage, looking for the main idea and the tone. That helps you stay focused. Keep asking yourself, "What are the main idea and the tone?" Don't try to memorize details, and don't reread hard lines. If you need them, you'll reread them later when you know the question and what to look for.

☐ **Skill 3.** To answer a "most nearly means" question, reread a few lines before the question and a few lines after it, and remember that the answer is usually not the most common definition.

☐ **Skill 4.** For a "direct info" question, always read before and after a line and find proof.

☐ **Skill 5.** For "suggest" questions, look for the answer that is hinted at in the passage; although it might use different language, it should be pretty close to what is actually said.

☐ **Skill 6.** For an "assumption" question, use the process of elimination.

☐ **Skill 7.** Answer "attitude" questions based on evidence in the passage; an author's attitude is expressed through his or her choice of words and punctuation.

☐ **Skill 8.** When there are two passages, read the first passage for the main idea and the tone and answer any questions that ask about Passage 1. Then read the second passage for the main idea and the tone and answer questions about that passage. Finally, answer questions that compare and contrast the two passages.

☐ **Skill 9.** If you need help with a "main idea" question, reread the intro paragraph and the first and last lines of each paragraph.

☐ **Skill 10.** For "best evidence" questions, read the four options and decide which one actually answers the previous question. That's your answer, AND it gives you the evidence you need for the previous question as well.

☐ **Skill 11.** Don't get intimidated by questions that refer to a table or graph. Treat them like any other question—find the evidence and use the process of elimination.

☐ **Skill 12.** When quotes around a phrase are not used to literally quote something from another source, they indicate that the phrase is being used in an unusual way, such as ironically. And words in parentheses usually function as a side note to the reader.

☐ **Skill 13.** For a "parallel" question, don't get thrown if the choices are not from the passage. Stay relaxed and focused, and look for the choice that proves or disproves the statement.

> Here's the question from the Pretest.
>
> **14.** In line 19, "this change" refers to
>
> (A) the beginning and end of the Vietnam War.
> (B) the different representations depicted in the two films.
> (C) the loss of American values.
> (D) the changing role of film in society.

Solution: This is a "direct info" question. Just read a few lines before and a few lines after "this change." The answer is evident in both sentences before and in one sentence after. Each demonstrates that "this change" specifically refers to the change in the depiction of American values as seen in the two films. Choice B is the best answer. Several other answers are close or have words that are recognizable from the passage, but they do not express the author's intention concerning "this change." Remember, the whole answer must work, not just the first few words.

Correct answer: B

> **How to Avoid the Six Most Common Careless Errors**
> **on SAT Reading Questions**
>
> 1. Don't select an answer based on just the first few words; the whole answer should make sense.
> 2. Be mindful on EXCEPT questions; you are looking for the choice that does not work.
> 3. Be mindful on LEAST/MOST questions.
> 4. Find evidence for your answer; be a lawyer.
> 5. Use evidence from the passage, not your own outside knowledge or opinions.
> 6. Don't get intimidated. If it seems hard, look for the evidence, decide what type of question it is, use your Mantras, and remember:
>   SAT Crashers Rule #45: No excuses. Test like a champion!

How to Be a Reading Ninja Drills

Identify each question type, and then choose the best answer.

The following passage examines certain themes of the Disney movie The Little Mermaid.

Among the most important themes in *The Little Mermaid* are those of questioning conventional thinking and pursuing a dream. Not only is Ariel, the little mermaid, demonstrating original
5 thought (something that many seem to think she is lacking), but she is rebelling against her speciesist father. When Ariel expresses her love for the human prince, King Trident is furious. When Ariel points out angrily that he does not
10 understand her, or even know the man whom she loves, Trident retorts, "Know him? I don't need to know him! He's a human!" In a very real way Disney is encouraging children to question preconceived ideas that we may have
15 against a certain group.

Disney also teaches children to pursue what they love. We see that Ariel's love for Prince Eric is more important than all else. In turning to the Sea Witch, Ursula, for help, Ariel makes a
20 mistake, but no true hero or heroine is flawless. Ariel puts herself, her family, and all merfolk in danger, but we see that with the help of her prince, she is able to put everything to rights.

At the end of the film, when Ursula has forced
25 King Trident to sacrifice his kingdom for his daughter's soul, the Sea Witch rises out of the water, gigantic and terrifying, wearing the king's crown and holding his magic trident. She laughs evilly and declares that she is the ruler
30 of all mermen and women. "So much for true love!" she screams victoriously. Eric, how- ever, succeeds in piloting the prow of his ship straight through her belly, vanquishing her. The moral here is that while we all make mistakes,
35 what is truly important is how we right the wrongs we may do to others.

1 The author's main point in the passage is that

(A) Ariel should not have been allowed to marry Prince Eric.

(B) only Prince Eric truly understood Ariel.

(C) Ariel demonstrated original thought.

(D) *The Little Mermaid* teaches children to follow their hearts.

2 Why does the author use parentheses around the comment in lines 5 to 6?

(A) To indicate a side comment to the reader

(B) To indicate that it is unimportant

(C) To indicate a humorous tone

(D) To indicate a shift in meaning

3 In line 7, Ariel's father is called "speciesist" because he

(A) does not know Eric.

(B) is king of his people and pursuing what he loves.

(C) is rebelling against preconceived notions.

(D) opposes Ariel's love based only on Eric's being human.

4 Which fictional plot line would best illustrate the assertion made in lines 13 to 15 ("Disney is . . . group.")?

(A) A movie about a boy who hates donkeys

(B) A movie about the development of the iPod

(C) A movie about a girl who overcomes her fear of snakes

(D) A movie that details the horrors of war

5 Ursula's quote in lines 30 and 31 primarily suggests that

(A) the marriage was unacceptable to her.

(B) she is mocking true love.

(C) she is speciesist.

(D) she was hurt in a prior relationship.

6 In line 33, "vanquishing" most nearly means

(A) loving.

(B) succeeding.

(C) besting.

(D) squashing.

7 The author's attitude toward *The Little Mermaid* is primarily one of

(A) frustration.

(B) stoicism.

(C) wonder.

(D) respect.

Alternate Nostril Breathing and Meditation

Alternate Nostril Breathing

This is a sweet technique. It will calm your mind and help you think clearly. And in yoga circles, it's considered a fast track to enlightenment. See, mom was right—SAT prep can fulfill all your dreams!

To try it, sit in a chair or on a cushion. Sit up straight, but relaxed. Bring your right hand to your nose. With your thumb, close the right nostril and inhale through the left. Then, with your pinky and ring finger, close your left nostril and exhale slowly through the right. A slow, relaxed exhalation. Then, still covering the left nostril, inhale through the right.

Then cover the right, and exhale slowly through the left. Inhale left, and switch. Continue alternating between right and left nostrils for several minutes. Slow, relaxed, deep, comfortable breaths.

According to yoga philosophy, you should end this practice with an exhale through the left nostril, then allow your breathing to return to normal.

Meditation

Running builds your endurance. Bench-pressing builds your pecs. Sit-ups tone your abs. Similarly, meditation builds your concentration "muscles" and strengthens your ability to stay focused.

How do you strengthen your concentration? It's easy, although, like weight lifting, it takes work and repetition. If you do the following exercise 5 minutes every morning and every night, I guarantee that you will build your ability to focus. This will make doing your homework easier, improve your grades, and bring up your SAT score. It will probably even improve your social life.

Here's how to meditate. Sit in a comfortable position on a chair or a cushion. You need not imitate a swami with your legs twisted together. Then close your eyes. Relax your face. Relax your body. Sit up straight, but relaxed. Become aware of your breathing. Find a spot where you notice your breathing, either the rise and fall of your belly or the in and out movement of air through your nostrils. Bring your attention to this place. Now, count 10 normal breaths. Unless you are already a Zen monk or a superhero, your mind will probably wander. That's okay. You'll start counting, "One, two, three, . . ." and then wander off and think about breakfast, the SATs, or yesterday's game. Whenever you notice that your mind has wandered, gently come back to counting the breaths. Start over at 1. If you ever make it to 10, start over at 1. Do this for 5 minutes.

Five minutes of this every morning and every night will change your life. Your concentration will improve. Your grades will go up. Your SAT score will go up. Your stress level will go down. It's a win-win.

Writing Multiple-Choice

The SAT contains a 35-minute Writing and Language section. The questions in this section test your ability to recognize and correct 20 kinds of grammatical errors. In the next 21 Skills, I will show you exactly what you need to know. I will show you how to recognize each type of error and how to correct it. Each Skill has an SAT Mantra. The Mantra tells you what to look for and what to do. Learn these Mantras and your score will go way up, guaranteed!

By the way, in the Writing and Language section, there are four passages, each with 11 questions. Some kids don't read the passages; they skip them and go right to the questions. But my students always gain points when they read the passage first. Even though you are not being tested on reading comprehension, sometimes you need the context.

With many writing multiple-choice questions, you'll know the error when you hear it. If something sounds wrong, it probably is. If something is difficult to read, it's probably wrong. The purpose of good grammar is to make writing easy to read and understand, so if it's not, if it trips up your tongue or if you can't get its meaning, don't say, "Boy, I can't do this." Say, "I can't understand this, so it must be bad grammar." Notice where your tongue gets tied up, where you have to pause and say, "What the . . . ?" That's where the error is, and there's your answer.

**When something trips up your tongue or you
can't get its meaning, it's probably wrong.**

For questions where your ear can't pick up the answer, we have Skills. Many kids who wind up scoring 700 or more on the Writing section started out saying, "I suck at these." I don't know where this attitude comes from. Maybe the way grammar is taught in school makes it seem very hard, or maybe it's not taught at all, but either way, on the SAT, these questions area easy and totally predicable! The SAT has chosen only a few concepts to test. Memorize these concepts in the next 21 Skills, and your score will go way up, guaranteed!

15 Subject/Verb Agreement

This is one of the most common types of SAT writing questions, and it's very easy. Basically, in a sentence, subject and verb must match. There is no fancy rule that I need to teach you; you already know this stuff just from speaking and reading. What I need to teach you is to train and then trust your ear, and, when in doubt, to identify the subject of the verb. In this Skill, we'll look at some straightforward questions. Then in Skill 16, we'll look at the two tricks that the SAT tries.

Let's take a look at this on the Pretest.

It was a Monday morning in 2006, and I $\underset{15}{\underline{\text{am}}}$ Kyle Tucker.

15. (A) NO CHANGE
    (B) was
    (C) were
    (D) have been

Solution: Trust your ear. "It was a Monday morning in 2006, and I <u>am</u> Kyle Tucker" does not sound correct. "It was Monday" implies that "I am" should be in the past tense: "I was." You can hear that if you know to listen for it. That's our goal: to train you to listen for it.

Correct answer: B

> **SAT Reading/Writing Mantra #15**
> When a verb is underlined, trust your ear. When in doubt, identify its subject and make sure that the singular/plural and tense match the subject.

Subject/Verb Agreement Drills

There is something delightfully bizarre in the art of improvisational theater. Not only being it completely unexpected and full of anxious excitement, but oftentimes, the material that emerges is utterly ridiculous.

For me, improv was hard at first. And scary. I been in organized productions since I was seven and had since then conquered stage fright. However, before my first improv performances, my heart would race the way it did when I were seven.

The nervousness that came from not knowing what I would say resulted in me groping about wildly.

This, I learned, will not earn you the laughter of the audience. What will work, however, are disregarding any preconceptions you have about having to be funny all the time, and letting yourself actually be listening and react to those around you.

1. (A) NO CHANGE
   (B) being
   (C) is it
   (D) it

2. (A) NO CHANGE
   (B) were
   (C) began to be
   (D) had being

3. (A) NO CHANGE
   (B) had been
   (C) will have been
   (D) was

4. (A) NO CHANGE
   (B) would have been
   (C) have been
   (D) was

5. (A) NO CHANGE
   (B) said
   (C) would have said
   (D) would have been saying

6. (A) NO CHANGE
   (B) being
   (C) is
   (D) has been

7. (A) NO CHANGE
   (B) listen and react
   (C) listens and reacts
   (D) listen and be reacting

Subject/Verb Agreement Tricks

The SAT can be tricky, but we know and expect its shenanigans. It's like a bad magician whose tricks you can totally predict. The SAT loves two kinds of subject/verb agreement tricks. Every test has at least one of them, but we expect them, so they're easy for us.

We saw the first trick on the Pretest.

I, with several other interns, <u>were arriving</u> at the "Bermuda Government Offices."
16

16. (A) NO CHANGE
(B) had been arrived
(C) was arriving
(D) were being arriving

Solution: I love these questions: they are tricky, but we know they are coming! The trick is that "interns" might look like the subject of the underlined verb, but "I" is actually the subject. "Interns **were** arriving" sounds correct, but the subject of the verb is "I," so it should be "I **was** arriving."

Correct answer: C

"How can I ever tell that?" you say. Ahh, my friend, that's easy. A prepositional phrase, such as "with his closest friends," NEVER counts as the subject. Prepositional phrases always begin with a preposition ("on," "above," "below," "with," "by," "during," "until," . . . just Google "prepositions" for a full list) and end with a noun, such as "friends." Here are a few more prepositional phrases: "of awards," "with six kids," and "on the table."

So when you are identifying the subject of an underlined verb, if there is a prepositional phrase, cross it out! Then the subject/verb agreement is obvious, and a "hard" question becomes easy!

Jimmy ~~with his friends~~ walks
The number ~~of awards~~ proves
Billy ~~along with six kids~~ goes

The SAT's other trick is to put the subject after the verb. How do you catch these? When you see a verb underlined, look for its subject—notice what is doing the action of the verb. It's easy to tell, as long as you know to look. I love these; they are tricky, but we know they are coming!

> **SAT Reading/Writing Mantra #16**
> When a verb is underlined, identify the subject and cross out any prepositional phrases; a prepositional phrase NEVER counts as the subject of the verb.
> Also, ask what is doing the action of the verb and watch for the second trick, where the subject comes after the verb.

Subject/Verb Agreement Tricks Drills

In each of the following sentences, cross out any prepositional phrases between the subject and the verb, and underline the subject of the bold verb.

1. Stephen ~~for two more weeks~~ **is** single.
2. Margarita ~~with her sisters~~ currently **runs** a marketing firm.
3. Running from the bulls **is** Jimmy ~~with his friends.~~
4. The way ~~of samurais~~ **is** a strict path.
5. ~~Around the corner~~ **are** a dog and a cat. *Compound subject*
6. The PTA ~~through generous donations~~ **is** building a new school building.
7. The boys ~~with their dog~~ Alfred **walk** to school.

Now, let's see these tricks on a few SAT questions.

Grandma's procedure for baking $\underline{\text{cookies have}}$ been written in my mind with dough and colored
$$\overline{1}$$
sugar.

After the sticks of butter $\underline{\text{have softened}}$, mix with
$$\overline{1}$$
one cup of sugar. Next, crack two eggs over the edge of the bowl and toss the shells into the compost bin. Add one teaspoon of vanilla. Then, one-half cup of brown and white sugars $\underline{\text{is}}$ added, and
$$\overline{3}$$
stir. Add two cups of flour, one teaspoon of salt, and one teaspoon of baking soda, and stir. Then place the dough in the freezer for one hour to harden. When the cookies, baking on the middle rack of the oven, $\underline{\text{becomes ready}}$, your nose will tell you.
$$\overline{4}$$

1.
   - Ⓐ NO CHANGE
   - Ⓑ cookies; have
   - Ⓒ cookies has
   - Ⓓ cookies being

2.
   - Ⓐ NO CHANGE
   - Ⓑ has softened
   - Ⓒ were soft
   - Ⓓ has been softened

3.
   - Ⓐ NO CHANGE
   - Ⓑ is being
   - Ⓒ will have been
   - Ⓓ are

4.
   - Ⓐ NO CHANGE
   - Ⓑ become ready
   - Ⓒ had become ready
   - Ⓓ was

Pronoun Clarity and Agreement

When a pronoun (such as "he," "she," "it," "they," "them," "him," or "her") is underlined, we must be totally sure what noun it is referring to. If this is unclear in any way, it is incorrect. You're smart, so you might be able to figure out which noun a pronoun refers to, but ask yourself, "If someone from another planet were translating this sentence, what would he think?" If it's at all unclear, it's wrong. Also, once you know what the pronoun refers to, make sure that it matches—singular or plural.

> Let's see this on the question from the Pretest.
>
> I approached the bulletin board that held your summer destiny. Jostling amongst other eager
> $\qquad$ 17
> students, my eyes read the dreadful words "Kyle Tucker—Assistant to the Assistant to the Assistant Secretary of Security Services."
>
> **17.** (A) NO CHANGE
> (B) one's
> (C) my
> (D) whose

Solution: We cannot be sure whom "your" refers to, so it's wrong. Also, on the SAT, you use "you" or "your" only if it is used consistently throughout the essay, and you never switch between "you" and "one."

Correct answer: C

As you learn these Skills, use them to analyze each underlined word. If the underlined word is a verb, ask, What is its subject? If it's a pronoun, ask, What does it refer to, and does it match?

> **SAT Reading/Writing Mantra #17**
> When a pronoun is underlined, we must be totally sure what noun it is referring to. If this is unclear in any way, the pronoun is incorrect. The underlined pronoun must also match (singular or plural) the noun that it refers to.

Here Are Most of the Pronouns That the SAT Uses		
All	I	Some
Both	It	Them
Each	Many	These
Few	Neither	They
He	Nobody	We
Her	None	Who
Him	One	You
His	She	Me

Pronoun Clarity and Agreement Drills

My grandma begins to flatten the dough with a wooden roller coated with flour. I devote my energies to the cookie cutters. <u>It is</u> all heaped
<u> </u>1
together in an old plastic shopping bag. I become

overwhelmed by my options and lay <u>them</u> all out.
2
I love the simplicity of the star, but am also

intrigued by the complexity of the Santa. There's also the reindeer, the Christmas tree, and the sleigh.

I select <u>those</u> cookie cutter that we will use and
3
realize I have chosen mostly stars and Santas.

My next task is to decorate the newly born shapes with sugar. <u>She</u> takes a step back from the table
4
and watches my eyes widen with excitement. I begin to sprinkle red and green sugar arbitrarily across the top of <u>each</u> cookie. I release the crystals
5
from my hand, and wherever <u>it ends</u> up is fine with
6
me. When I finally finish, my grandma tells me that they are "just perfect" and places them in the oven.

1. Ⓐ NO CHANGE
   Ⓑ It
   Ⓒ They being
   Ⓓ They are

2. Ⓐ NO CHANGE
   Ⓑ it
   Ⓒ each one
   Ⓓ those

3. Ⓐ NO CHANGE
   Ⓑ their
   Ⓒ each
   Ⓓ these

4. Ⓐ NO CHANGE
   Ⓑ My grandma
   Ⓒ He
   Ⓓ Who

5. Ⓐ NO CHANGE
   Ⓑ each and every
   Ⓒ this
   Ⓓ which

6. Ⓐ NO CHANGE
   Ⓑ those end
   Ⓒ they end
   Ⓓ those released crystals ends

Correct Transition Word

When a transition word (such as "although," "since," "but," "therefore," or "however") is underlined, see if it works in the flow of the sentence. Words like "therefore" express a direct cause and effect. Opposition words like "but" express a cause and effect in which the second part opposes the first. For example:

Brian is funny; <u>therefore</u>, he makes you laugh.
    The second part results from the first part.
Brian is funny, <u>but</u> sometimes he is tired and dull.
    The second part opposes the first part.

When a transition word is underlined, check whether it's the right transition word for the sentence. These are great. If you didn't know to look for them, you might miss 'em. You might think, "That was weird, but I guess it's okay." But it's not okay.

Let's take a look at the one from the Pretest.

"No, No, No!" I thought. <u>Nevertheless</u>, I got angry—blood rushed to my head and my knees went weak.   18

18. (A) NO CHANGE
    (B) But,
    (C) Still
    (D) OMIT the underlined portion.

Solution: "I got angry" follows the flow of the paragraph, rather than opposing it. However, "nevertheless" implies opposition, so we want a different transition word, such as "therefore." All the choices are opposition words, so choice D (OMIT the underlined portion) is correct.

Correct answer: D
If we weren't looking for this, we might miss it, but we are expecting it, and so we catch it. This is where my job is easy; I just tell you what to look out for. Then you get them right, and it makes me look good!

SAT Reading/Writing Mantra #18
When a transition word (such as "although," "since," "but," "therefore," or "however") is underlined, see whether it works in the sentence.

Direct Cause-and-Effect Words			*Opposition Words*		
Therefore	Thus	So	However	Although	But
Ergo	And	Since	Still	Though	
Because			Nevertheless	Even though	

Correct Transition Word Drills

Catherine the Great became empress of Russia in 1769. She guided Russia in a Golden Age for 34 years. Otherwise, this Golden Age was indeed

1
a time of prosperity for many, for others it was a time of oppression.

To many it appeared that Catherine was guiding Russia into prosperity, though, underneath the

2
surface, she disregarded the underprivileged. She took away their land and made it difficult for them to acquire an education. Since Catherine is known

3
as a just ruler, under her reign the peasantry actually suffered greatly.

Whereas Catherine effected many advancements

4
during her reign, such as founding the Russian Academy; however, these achievements targeted the nobility. For example, the schools she founded

5
were private with very expensive tuition. While Catherine did bring the Renaissance to Russia, peasants were too busy working to benefit from it. In truth, Catherine the Great took advantage of many to benefit the few, therefore.

6

1. (A) NO CHANGE
   (B) Therefore
   (C) Although
   (D) And,

2. (A) NO CHANGE
   (B) for
   (C) therefore
   (D) moreover

3. (A) NO CHANGE
   (B) While
   (C) Because
   (D) Thus,

4. (A) NO CHANGE
   (B) Since
   (C) Considering
   (D) DELETE the underlined portion.

5. (A) NO CHANGE
   (B) Yet,
   (C) Because of
   (D) But,

6. (A) NO CHANGE
   (B) few
   (C) few of them
   (D) few, yet

Brave, Honest, and Relaxed

Words in a list must match. The fancy name for this is "parallel structure," but we don't need that term for the SAT. Your ear can tell you if the words match, as long as you watch for it. That's the key on so many of these Skills. You already know the material; you just need to practice watching for it.

Look at these examples:

These match:
- When I traveled cross-country, I followed the motto, "**brave, honest, and relaxed**."
- Sanaa is **beautiful, funny, and kind**.
- Omar will **run, jump, and swim**.
- To test the endurance of their warriors, the ancient Spartans held contests involving **running, fighting, and enduring** pain.

These do not match:
- When I traveled cross-country, I followed the motto, "**brave, honest, and <u>be relaxed</u>**."
- Sanaa is **beautiful, funny, and <u>acts kindly</u>**.
- Omar **runs, jumps, and <u>will swim</u>**.
- To test the endurance of their warriors, the ancient Spartans held contests involving **running, fighting, and to <u>endure</u>** pain.

In this last example, the first two members of the list do not have the "to" in front of them. All members of the list must match. Either they all have a "to" or none do. It's like bringing cupcakes to school in third grade—either you have enough for everyone or you don't bring 'em!

Let's apply this on the Pretest.

I considered protesting, having a tantrum, and <u>I considered quitting</u> .
19

19. (A) NO CHANGE
(B) I just plain considered quitting
(C) quitting
(D) considering quitting

Solution: Easy; when you have a list, all the words must match. The list here is "protesting, having a tantrum, and I considered quitting." The first two parts match ("protesting" and "having a tantrum"), but the third part, "I considered quitting," does not match. So the third part must be simply "quitting."

Correct answer: C

> **SAT Reading/Writing Mantra #19**
> **When words in a list are underlined, make sure they match.**

Brave, Honest, and Relaxed Drills

Let's look at a few specific examples of this.

1 The storm tore through the new forest, uprooting saplings, leveling huts, and <u>animals' homes were disturbed</u>.

- Ⓐ NO CHANGE
- Ⓑ animals' homes disturbing
- Ⓒ animals' homes disturbed
- Ⓓ disturbing animals' homes

2 Ian's four weeks at language school <u>had been interesting, informative, and had opened his eyes</u>; he gained new insights and a new appreciation of relationships.

- Ⓐ NO CHANGE
- Ⓑ were interesting and informative, and had opened his eyes
- Ⓒ had been interesting, informative, and eye-opening
- Ⓓ had been interesting, informative, and opened his eyes

3 A skilled and versatile musician, Satyajit has been a guitarist, vocalist, drummer, <u>and worked as a soundman</u>.

- Ⓐ NO CHANGE
- Ⓑ and soundman
- Ⓒ and working as a soundman
- Ⓓ and has worked as a soundman

4 This book will help you confidently answer reading comprehension questions, writing multiple-choice questions, and <u>to write the essay</u>.

- Ⓐ NO CHANGE
- Ⓑ writing the essay
- Ⓒ the essay
- Ⓓ to write

5 Now Kathy feels healthy, grounded and <u>is ready to broaden</u> her environment.

- Ⓐ NO CHANGE
- Ⓑ ready to broaden
- Ⓒ the readiness for broadening
- Ⓓ a broadening readiness

6 Every mathematician must master the basic skills of <u>addition, multiplication, and subtracting</u> before moving on to more involved operations.

- Ⓐ NO CHANGE
- Ⓑ adding, multiplication, and subtracting
- Ⓒ addition, multiplication, and to subtract
- Ⓓ addition, multiplication, and subtraction

Comparison

In Skill 19, I taught you that words in a list must match; similarly, words that are being compared must match. There are three ways that this shows up on the SAT.

- **Doing** yoga is as cool as **acing** the SAT.
- **John's singing** is better than **Ed's**.
- Aunt Frances is not only **smart**, but also **athletic**.

Let's take a look at the question from the Pretest.

My skills were far stronger than $\underline{\text{the guy who got the job I wanted}}_{20}$.

20. (A) NO CHANGE
    (B) that guy
    (C) the other guy
    (D) those of the guy who got the job I wanted

Solution: Great question. Nearly every SAT has one like this. Most kids get it wrong; if you know to look for it, you'll get it right! The problem with the sentence is that it compares "my skills" with "the other guy." It should compare skills to skills or person to person, so in this case, "My skills are far stronger than those of the other guy."

Correct answer: D

SAT Reading/Writing Mantra #20
When words being compared are underlined, make sure they match.

Comparison Drills

Let's practice with a few specific examples.

1 Anyone <u>who has extra time or great interest</u> can
   1
learn the tricks and illusions that a successful
magician needs.

  Ⓐ NO CHANGE

  Ⓑ who has extra time or is in fact very
     interested

  Ⓒ who has extra time or very interest

  Ⓓ who has extra time or who has interested

2 Because they paint for fun, rather than <u>for
profiting</u> many young painters particularly
  2
enjoy their craft.

  Ⓐ NO CHANGE

  Ⓑ for profit

  Ⓒ to profit from it

  Ⓓ for the profiting

3 One day, David will be known not only as an
honored graduate of Harvard University, but
also <u>he writes many important</u> works of American fiction.   3

  Ⓐ NO CHANGE

  Ⓑ he then will write many important

  Ⓒ will he write many important

  Ⓓ as an author who writes many important

4 Businesses rely more on consumer <u>spending
than do they rely on government subsidies</u> to
  4
meet their yearly expenditures.

  Ⓐ NO CHANGE

  Ⓑ spending than them relying on government
     subsidies

  Ⓒ spending than on government subsidies

  Ⓓ spending than businesses rely on govern-
     ment subsidies

5 Bill Bryson's book *A Walk in the Woods* is funnier
and more widely read than <u>Karl Marx</u>.
  5

  Ⓐ NO CHANGE

  Ⓑ is Karl Marx

  Ⓒ Karl Marx is

  Ⓓ Karl Marx's *The Communist Manifesto*

Relaxing Commas

Most kids see commas as a great mystery. But commas follow rules. They just indicate a pause; they are very relaxing. So when a comma is underlined on the SAT, ask yourself, Should there be a pause here? Use your ear—read the material with and without a pause and see which works.

When you need to double-check your ear, here are the comma rules for the SAT:

1   Use a comma to set off a side note.
    Example: This book, as you know, is quite excellent.
    You can hear the pause before and after the side note "as you know."
    Example: You, Matt, are a great pianist.
    You can hear the pause before and after the side note "Matt."
    These sentences would sound bizarre if you read them without the pauses.

2   Don't use a comma if a phrase is essential to the sentence, because then it's not a side note.
    Example: "The word 'facile'" comes from the Spanish word for easy.
    No commas because "the word 'facile'" is essential, not a side note. If we took it out, the sentence would lose its meaning.
    Plus, if you try pausing before and after it, it sounds weird.

There's one more rule that we need, which we'll look at in Skill 22.

Let's take a look at the question from the Pretest.

Not <u>me, the budding politician, an</u> assistant to the assistant of the assistant?
                        21

21. (A) NO CHANGE
      (B) me the budding politician an
      (C) me the budding politician an,
      (D) me the budding politician; an

Solution: Try it with and without pauses. With pauses, it sounds clear, and without pauses, it sounds confusing and jumbled. "The budding politician" is a side note, inessential to the meaning of the sentence, so we need the commas.

Correct answer: A

> **SAT Mantra #21**
> **When a comma is underlined on the SAT, ask yourself, Should there be a**
> **pause here? Read it with and without a pause and see which works.**
> **Commas (and pauses) are used to set off a side note.**

Relaxing Commas Drills

My Room My room, is always there for me. All my
 ‾‾‾‾‾
   1
things are there: the pictures, the books, the fold-
ers from fourth grade. The walls are covered with
 memories from my three-year-old birthday poster
 ‾‾‾‾‾‾‾
   2
to faded paintings done in seventh grade.

The rugs underfoot being always dusty,
        ‾‾‾‾‾‾‾‾‾‾‾‾
           3
always comforting, are a multicolor patchwork
 of irregular shapes. Out the window is a familiar
 ‾‾‾‾‾‾‾‾‾‾‾‾‾‾
     4
landscape, always there, like an old friend that
won't let me down. The colors of the wall blue and
                                    ‾‾‾‾‾‾‾‾
                                       5
red, are deep rich colors that warm me and keep me
safe. Sometimes, though like on hot days, the deep
               ‾‾‾‾‾‾
                  6
colors keep me cool.

The most special place in the whole room, my bed .
                                   ‾‾‾‾‾‾‾‾‾‾‾
                                        7
It's a place to relax and just be, a reassuring face in
a sometimes unfriendly world. The cozy blankets
are always ready to warm me; the pillow is a fluffy
cloud. My room is a special world all of my own.

1 (A) NO CHANGE
    (B) room,
    (C) room is,
    (D) room is

2 (A) NO CHANGE
    (B) memories;
    (C) memories,
    (D) memories, and

3 (A) NO CHANGE
    (B) underfoot, really
    (C) underfoot are
    (D) underfoot,

4 (A) NO CHANGE
    (B) of, irregular, shapes
    (C) of, irregular shapes
    (D) of irregular, shapes

5 (A) NO CHANGE
    (B) wall is blue
    (C) wall, blue
    (D) wall, being blue

6 (A) NO CHANGE
    (B) therefore,
    (C) though;
    (D) though,

7 (A) NO CHANGE
    (B) room is my bed
    (C) room, being my bed
    (D) room; my bed

Are You Independent?

I told you in Skill 21 that there was one more comma rule for the SAT. Here it is. When a phrase in a sentence does not complete a thought but leaves you waiting for the rest, you separate it from the rest of the sentence with a comma (or a dash or parentheses). When the phrase is a complete thought that could stand on its own and does not leave you hanging, you separate it with a semicolon or a comma with "and."

The fancy term for a phrase that cannot stand alone is "dependent," and the fancy term for one that can is "independent." That makes sense, like when you have a job and learn to cook and can stand on your own, you are independent.

Commas, Dashes, Parentheses

He thought, as soon as he woke up, that he'd like to go back to sleep.
He thought—as soon as he woke up—that he'd like to go back to sleep.
He thought (as soon as he woke up) that he'd like to go back to sleep.

In all these examples, the phrase "as soon as he woke up" is dependent—it would not be a complete sentence alone. Therefore, it is separated by commas, dashes, or parentheses. Technically, each of these has a subtly different use, but the SAT uses them interchangeably and **never** tests the differences between commas, dashes, and parentheses.

Semicolon

He woke up; he decided to go back to bed.
He woke up, and he decided to go back to bed.
He woke up. He decided to go back to bed.

Both parts of each of these sentences are independent and could stand alone, so they are separated by a semicolon, a comma with "and," or a period.

Let's take a look at the question from the Pretest.

I found my <u>department, and I was</u> immediately given a list of mundane tasks.
            22

22. Which of the following alternatives to the underlined portion would NOT be acceptable?

   (A) department: and I was
   (B) department; I was
   (C) department and was
   (D) department. I was

Solution: "I found my department" and "I was immediately . . . " are both complete thoughts that could stand alone; they are independent. Therefore, they must be separated by a semicolon, a comma with "and," or a period. Using the process of elimination, choice A is the answer. I did not teach you about colons yet, so here goes: Colons are used to separate a list or a clause that explains. Choice A would work if the second part of the sentence expounded on the first and did not have the "and"; for example, "I found my department: it was the filing room."

Correct answer: A

> **SAT Mantra #22**
> **Phrases that can stand alone are separated with a semicolon,**
> **a comma with "and," or a period.**

Are You Independent? Drills

Jean Piaget popularized a theory of intellectual development; he taught that all children moved
_____1_____
through a set pattern of development in a fixed order. He called the four stages of development; the
_____2_____
sensorimotor, the preoperational, the concrete operational, and the formal operational.

Piaget's stages are often contrasted with those of Erik Erikson. Erikson focused on how children come to understand themselves. And,
_____3_____
the world around them. His theory has eight stages, beginning at birth and ending in late
_____4_____
adulthood.

The first four stages of Erikson's theory cover the same ages as Piaget's four stages; however, other
_____5_____
than age of experience, the stages do not have an obvious relationship to each other.

1. Which of the following alternatives to the underlined portion would NOT be acceptable?
   - (A) development. He taught that
   - (B) development—that
   - (C) development; teaching that
   - (D) development, teaching that

2. (A) NO CHANGE
   - (B) development the
   - (C) development, the
   - (D) development; as the

3. (A) NO CHANGE
   - (B) themselves; and
   - (C) themselves,
   - (D) themselves and

4. (A) NO CHANGE
   - (B) stages; and begins
   - (C) stages, it begins
   - (D) stages; beginning

5. (A) NO CHANGE
   - (B) stages, however, other
   - (C) stages, however. Other
   - (D) stages, however; other

Correct Preposition

The SAT calls this topic "correct idiom." I love this term; you just don't hear people using the word "idiom" nearly enough. It makes me think of *Monty Python and the Holy Grail* when Sir Lancelot receives a call of distress from the singing Prince of Swamp Castle. Lancelot's squire wants to come along for the daring rescue, but Lancelot says that he must rush the castle "in his own particular . . . idiom."

However, instead of "correct idiom," which I can't say without laughing, I call this skill "correct preposition." I do this for two reasons:

1 I'm not sure if I'd have to pay the SAT to use its term.

2 The words that we are looking for are always prepositions, so finding them is much easier than looking for the "correct idiom."

Remember from Skill 16 that prepositions are words like "up," "above," "of," "into," "on," "below," "with," "by," "during," and "until." You can Google "prepositions" for a full list. When a preposition is underlined, ask yourself if it's the correct preposition. How do you know? The correct one will make sense and sound smooth. The wrong one will sound weird or jarring. This is another great place to practice trusting your ear. If a preposition sounds jarring, it's probably wrong. We'll train on this in the drills.

Here are some examples:

Correct:	Incorrect
Zann went **to** the movies.	Zann went **onto** the movies.
Giancarlo sat **on** the couch.	Giancarlo sat **in** the couch.
Malaria is a threat **to** travelers.	Malaria is a threat **of** travelers.
Focusing **on** your studies will bring you success.	Focusing **with** your studies will bring you success.

Let's practice on the question from the Pretest.

I was young, but I understood every aspect <u>in the government</u>.
                                                            23

23. (A) NO CHANGE
    (B) the government offered
    (C) of the government
    (D) for the government

Solution: "But I understood every aspect in the government" sounds weird. The aspects are not literally **in** the government; they are aspects **of** the government. "Every aspect of the government" sounds great. Trust your ear. This is a great Skill; knowing to watch for the correct preposition turns a hard question into easy points!

Correct answer: C

SAT Mantra #23
When a preposition is underlined, ask yourself if it is the right preposition to use.

Correct Preposition Drills

Feeling out of place at school and needing something new, last January, I started helping out on
<u>1</u>

Miss Kelly's study halls. Every Tuesday and Thursday, I'd read novels to eighth graders. If I continued <u>in reading</u> the same page over and
<u>2</u>

over again enough times, they'd understand it.

One day the science teacher told me, beaming, that one of my students had received a B <u>on</u> his ecosystems and biomes test.
<u>3</u>

That student, Nick, never said a word <u>on</u> it to
<u>4</u>

me, even though he and I had spent a long time studying the material together. Truthfully, I don't know if he even cared <u>for</u> the grade, but I had never been prouder. <u>5</u>

Tutoring those kids turned out <u>on being</u> one of the
<u>6</u>

most rewarding experiences I had ever had. I still felt a little out of place at school, but I had a purpose, and I was excited when I woke up every day, especially on Tuesdays and Thursdays.

1. (A) NO CHANGE
   (B) out to
   (C) out in
   (D) out into

2. (A) NO CHANGE
   (B) to read
   (C) on reading
   (D) the reading of

3. (A) NO CHANGE
   (B) with
   (C) about
   (D) in

4. (A) NO CHANGE
   (B) by
   (C) for
   (D) about

5. (A) NO CHANGE
   (B) about
   (C) what
   (D) on

6. (A) NO CHANGE
   (B) in being
   (C) for
   (D) to be

It's Me

The SAT likes "me." It also loves "I." The people there love to ask you whether "I" or "me" is correct in a sentence. That's great, because we have an incredibly easy and effective way to determine which is correct. If "I" or "me" is underlined, test it by putting it first or dropping the other person and then trusting your ear. You can also use this trick for "who" versus "whom," "he" versus "him," etc.

The second special pronoun that the SAT loves to test is "its" versus "it's." Usually, apostrophe s ('s) means possession, as in "Brian's book." But "it's" is a special case; it means the contraction for "it is," while "its" is possessive, like "its color is red."

"It's" means "It is."
"Its" is possessive, like "that tree is nice; I like **its** colorful leaves."

That's it. Drill and memorize these, and you'll gain points.

Let's try this on the question from the Pretest.

At some point before midday, I began thinking seriously about quitting. "The Assistant's office, its right downstairs," I thought.
    24

24. (A) NO CHANGE
    (B) office; its
    (C) office, it's
    (D) office

Solution: First, this is a great review of Skill 22. "The assistant's office" is not complete; it cannot stand alone. So it must have a comma instead of a semicolon. Second, "its" is possessive, but we want the contraction for "it is," so choice C is correct.

Correct answer: C

SAT Mantra #24
If "I" or "me" is underlined, test it by putting the I/me first or drop the other person and trust your ear. If "its" or "it's" is underlined, remember that "it's" means "it is" and "its" is possessive, like "that tree is nice; I like <u>its</u> colorful leaves."

Our "Put the I/me first or drop the other person and trust your ear" strategy also applies to

I vs. me
He vs. him
She vs. her
We vs. us
They vs. them
Who vs. whom

It's Me Drills

Sometime in college, Manuel and me had heard
                     ——————————
                          1
that an enlightened person is so relaxed that their
eyes are always half closed. I doubt its true , but at
                                       ————
                                          2
the time we believed it.

A few years later we were traveling and met a guru,
a very advanced yoga teacher. "The key to a yoga
practice," he said, "is to follow its call." We all sat
                                    ———
                                     3
together awhile and talked.

The scene was perfect. Someone brought tea to
Manuel and I . The guru wore all white and
——————————
      4
sandals and spoke in wise aphorisms.

I was listening to a story about he and his student
                                 ————————————
                                       5
when I realized that the guru's eyes were half
closed. "Wow," I thought, "he is enlightened."

Later, when I was about to leave, I said, "I'd love to
attend one of your yoga classes." "That would be
wonderful," he responded, "except, I'm not teaching this month. I just had eye surgery, and who
                                            ———
                                             6
can see with these darn drops in their eyes!"

1. Ⓐ NO CHANGE
   Ⓑ Manuel and I,
   Ⓒ Manuel and I
   Ⓓ me and Manuel

2. Ⓐ NO CHANGE
   Ⓑ if there is truthfulness to this
   Ⓒ it's true
   Ⓓ its the truth

3. Ⓐ NO CHANGE
   Ⓑ it's
   Ⓒ their
   Ⓓ they're

4. Ⓐ NO CHANGE
   Ⓑ Manuel and myself
   Ⓒ Manuel and, I
   Ⓓ Manuel and me

5. Ⓐ NO CHANGE
   Ⓑ his student and himself
   Ⓒ him and his student
   Ⓓ his student and he

6. Ⓐ NO CHANGE
   Ⓑ whom
   Ⓒ which person
   Ⓓ whose

A Few More Rules

Each of the writing Skills that you've learned so far appears on almost every SAT. The four topics in this Skill appear less often, but often enough that you should memorize them.

1 Apostrophes
Examples: the teacher's book—one teacher has a book
the teachers' book—more than one teacher possesses the book
Remember from Skill 24 that "its" is possessive and "it's" means "it is."
Also, "who's" means "who is" and "whose" is possessive.

2 "-er" vs. "-est"
Use "more" or "-er" when comparing two things.
Use "most" or "-est" when comparing three or more things.
Examples: Of cats and dogs, dogs are the **lazier** animal.
Of all animals, cows are the **laziest.**
(P.C. notice: Neither the author nor the publisher believes that cows or dogs are lazy.)

3 "Which" is for things; "who" is for people.
Examples: Sierra is a girl **who** runs every day.
Computers are things **which** people love or hate.

4 Certain words go together, such as
Neither . . . nor
Either . . . or
Not only . . . but also
Example: I like **neither** ham **nor** venison.

Now, let's look at the example from the Pretest.

I saw my <u>mom's eyes and heard both of my uncles'</u> laughter.
                                    25

25. (A) NO CHANGE
(B) moms eyes and heard both of my uncles
(C) mom's eyes and heard both of my uncle's
(D) mom's eyes and heard both of my uncles

Solution: Since there are two uncles, "uncles' laughter" is correct. "Mom's" is also correct. So there is no error.

Correct answer: A

> **SAT Mantra #25**
> "My uncle's books" means that one uncle has books, and "my uncles' books" means that two or more uncles have the books. "-Er" or "more" is used to compare two things, and "-est" or "most" is used to compare more than two things. "Who" is for people, and "which" is for things. Watch for pairs of words such as "not only . . . but also" and "either . . . or."

A Few More Rules Drills

The Boredoms is one noise band <u>which</u> I've actually
₁
listened to. I can't say that I constantly walk around
with them in my earphones, but I'm somewhat
<u>familiarly</u> with their sound and have identified
₂
certain moments when they are just the thing.

What I admire about their project is that they can
not only deconstruct, <u>and</u> also reconstruct a song
₃
at will. Sometimes the sound devolves into arrhyth-
mic mutterings, and other times the disparate pieces
find one another and form something <u>their own</u> ,
₄
and a throbbing, perplexing song emerges.

While their sound is every bit as difficult as most
grind <u>groups sounds</u> , they are special for not tak-
₅
ing themselves so seriously. If you're going to do
crazy stuff like this, I'd say you should do it for fun.

1. Ⓐ NO CHANGE
   Ⓑ who
   Ⓒ whom
   Ⓓ whose

2. Ⓐ NO CHANGE
   Ⓑ familiarity
   Ⓒ familiar
   Ⓓ recognizable

3. Ⓐ NO CHANGE
   Ⓑ but
   Ⓒ yet
   Ⓓ while

4. Ⓐ NO CHANGE
   Ⓑ it's own;
   Ⓒ his own:
   Ⓓ whose own,

5. Ⓐ NO CHANGE
   Ⓑ group's sounds
   Ⓒ groups' sounds
   Ⓓ groups sound's

The SAT is not testing to see if you are the next William Shakespeare. It is merely testing to see if you can write a clear and concise memo from your cubicle at Dandar Mifflin Corporation.

Not that there's anything wrong with writing a clear and concise memo. In fact, whether you're the CEO of Sony or a published novelist, it's great to be able to write in a variety of styles—personal, creative, and professional. Then you can adjust your style to the task.

It's also helpful, on the SAT and in life, to know the rules and the expectations for the task. Imagine that Michael Jordan had never seen a hoop before. If you placed him on a court, he'd still have the potential to be the best ever, and yet he wouldn't even know how to score. Acknowledging rules and expectations gives you freedom and choice; you can choose whether you follow them, but at least the choice is yours.

So the secret rule for writing multiple-choice questions is to choose the answer that is the most clear, concise, direct, and nonredundant. Now, you can identify the best answer choice and be the Michael Jordan of the SAT.

Let's see this on the Pretest.

What I said to my <u>neighbor intern who worked next to me</u>, I don't recall.
26

26. (A) NO CHANGE
(B) neighbor intern next to me,
(C) neighbor intern
(D) neighbor, the intern next to me

Solution: The word "neighbor" implies the person "who worked next to me," so the other words are redundant and unneeded. Ax them. The SAT likes things crisp and clear. We always want the answer that is most clear, concise, direct, and nonredundant, and of course grammatically correct.

Correct answer: C

SAT Mantra #26
**The SAT likes things crisp and clear; we always want the answer
that is most clear, concise, direct, and nonredundant.**

Direct, to the Point, Not Redundant Drills

Begin to take deep, relaxed breaths, breathing in a relaxed way. Mentally
$\underline{\text{1}}$
scanning your body, consciously relax your muscles, one at a time, from your toes to the top of your head. Stress and tension are breathed out
$\underline{\text{2}}$
with each exhalation. With each inhalation, breathe in relaxation.

After your muscles have become relaxed, and less tight, allow your mind
$\underline{\text{3}}$
to relax. Notice anxieties and mental tensions. Visualize the incoming breath dissolving buried mental tensions. Then, imagining that your mind is like a clear blue sky, it is that you see the thoughts as slowly floating
$\underline{\text{4}}$
clouds.

Relax here awhile. Then, when you are ready and all set, gently stretch your body in the
$\underline{\text{5}}$
way that feels most natural for you. Notice how you feel and make the intention to return to this feeling whenever you need some stress relief. Then, open your eyes and with open eyes slowly sit up.
$\underline{\text{6}}$

1. (A) NO CHANGE
   (B) breaths, and breathing in a relaxed way.
   (C) breaths, in a relaxed way.
   (D) breaths.

2. (A) NO CHANGE
   (B) Let stress and tension be the things breathed out
   (C) Breathe out stress and tension
   (D) In the breathing, let it be stress and tension that are breathed out

3. (A) NO CHANGE
   (B) relaxed
   (C) relaxed, with less tension
   (D) relaxed, and are less tight

4. (A) NO CHANGE
   (B) it being that you are imagining that your mind is like a clear blue sky,
   (C) imagining that your mind is like a clear blue sky, you
   (D) imagine that your mind is like a clear blue sky and

5. (A) NO CHANGE
   (B) set and ready
   (C) all ready and set
   (D) ready

6. (A) NO CHANGE
   (B) with opened-eyes
   (C) with eyes being open
   (D) OMIT the underlined portion

Misplaced Phrases

Look at this sentence:

A beloved children's story, Ethel read "The Three Little Pigs" to her son.

The sentence makes it sound as if Ethel is a beloved children's story. That's how an alien from another planet would read this sentence. "A beloved children's story" is misplaced. It should be closer to the thing it's describing, "The Three Little Pigs." On the SAT, a descriptive phrase should always be very close to the thing that it describes. The SAT uses this type of question **several times** on each test.

Let's see this on the Pretest.

Climbing the metal stairs, <u>the intern supervisor's cubicle</u> was two flights up.
27

27. (A) NO CHANGE
    (B) the cubicle of the intern supervisor
    (C) I made a beeline to the intern supervisor's cubicle, which
    (D) the intern supervisors cubicle which

Solution: The way the sentence is set up, it seems as if "Climbing the metal stairs" is describing the intern supervisor's cubicle. Of course it is not; you're smart, and you know that, but someone translating the sentence would be misled. That's the point of good grammar: to make writing completely clear. So "Climbing the metal stairs" should be as close to the thing that it describes ("I") as possible, and choice C is the best. Choice C also makes the sentence more clear and direct.

This question is a great place to use the process of elimination. If you are ever confused by a question, identify an error that needs fixing and eliminate choices that don't fix the error. In this case, choices A, B, and D all have a misplaced phrase. Even if you can't identify choice C as the right answer, you can get it by the process of elimination!

Correct answer: C

SAT Mantra #27
A descriptive phrase on the SAT must be clearly associated with
(and usually placed right next to) the noun described.

Misplaced Phrases Drills

My grandparents'

<u>farm was the opposite of my apartment</u>
$\qquad\qquad\qquad\qquad$ 1

<u>in the city, with the fresh air of its open pasture</u> .
$\qquad\qquad\qquad\qquad$ 1

I remember eating early morning corn flakes with brown sugar and advising Grandpa on his game of solitaire. This was followed by midmorning

breakfast <u>with Grandma of Rice Krispies and toast</u>
$\qquad\qquad\qquad\qquad$ 2

<u>with plenty of jam</u> .
$\quad$ 2

Grandma and I would go to the neighborhood ladies' brunch, but first, we'd bring lunch pails <u>in the fields baling hay out to the workers</u>. Those
$\qquad\qquad\qquad\qquad$ 3
summers I learned to knit. I remember Grandma's limitless repertoire of knitting, embroidery, crochet, and sewing projects.

<u>I savored the familiar smell of</u> Grandpa's work
$\qquad\qquad\qquad$ 4
shirt. I remember his enormous hands and the lines that told the stories of decades of satisfying hard work.

<u>With rhythm and simplicity, the memory of the time</u>
$\qquad\qquad\qquad\qquad$ 5
I spent with Grandma and Grandpa gives me a sense of security, nurturing, and calm.

---

1. Ⓐ NO CHANGE

Ⓑ farm was like the opposite to my city apartment, and the fresh air of the open pasture

Ⓒ farm, was the opposite of my apartment in the city with the fresh air of the open pasture

Ⓓ farm, with the fresh air of its open pasture, was the opposite of my apartment in the city

2. Ⓐ NO CHANGE

Ⓑ of Rice Krispies and toast with plenty of jam of Grandma's.

Ⓒ with Grandma; we ate Rice Krispies and toast with plenty of jam

Ⓓ and Grandma's eating Rice Krispies and toast with plenty of jam

3. Ⓐ NO CHANGE

Ⓑ in the fields' hay baling out to the workers

Ⓒ out to the workers baling hay in the fields

Ⓓ out in the fields baling hay to the workers

4. Ⓐ NO CHANGE

Ⓑ With its familiar smell, I savored

Ⓒ With its smell, I familiarly savored

Ⓓ The familiar smell, I was always savoring

5. Ⓐ NO CHANGE

Ⓑ The memory of the rhythm and simplicity of the time

Ⓒ With rhythm and simplicity, the time of the memory

Ⓓ With rhythm and simplicity, I remember the time

Word Choice

In ninth grade, my best friend got hold of a thesaurus. Trying to impress our English teacher, he replaced a bunch of the words in his essay with fancier words. The problem was that the fancier words didn't always quite fit, and the essay sounded crazy.

The SAT loves to do that too. The developer just clicks on the thesaurus button and substitutes a word that means nearly the same thing, but does not fit in the sentence. This is definitely another "trust your ear" topic. If something sounds crazy, it is. Don't say, "That sounds kinda funny, but I must be wrong." Say, "That sounds weird, so let's see if the choices give something that sounds better." And if you have trouble with the vocabulary, revisit the Vocabulary Special Sections on pages 34–43.

Let's take a look at the question from the Pretest.

I remember staring at the man sitting there expectantly, the <u>curiously</u> look on his face, and then down at my hands, then at the Ministry exit doors.　28

28. (A) NO CHANGE
　　(B) quizzical
　　(C) stormy
　　(D) questionable

Solution: Your ear can definitely tell that "the <u>curiously</u> look" sounds weird and is wrong. This is actually a nice preview of Skill 32 "Sometimes the SAT adds an 'ly' that does not belong." This is tough to catch for someone who wasn't expecting it, but easy for us! So now that we know this, it sounds weird; let's see how the answers sound. Only choice B makes sense in the context of the paragraph. The man does not have a stormy (violently angry) or questionable (disputed) look on his face; he has a quizzical (inquiring) look.

Correct answer: B

SAT Mantra #28
Make sure that the underlined word fits into the context of the sentence.

Word Choice Drills

The hit TV show *Entourage* <u>demonstrates</u> a young
                              1
movie star navigating life in Hollywood. In the
show, the main character, Vince, faces <u>contests</u>
                                          2
from other actors to get the best roles. Yet, he
remains grounded and calm.

In one episode, when he was <u>known to</u> go on a late
                              3
night talk show, his advisors told him to prep interesting topics to discuss. But he just decided to go on
the show and be present. It's this very attitude that
makes him so successful with so <u>much</u> loyal fans.
                                   4

He is present to opportunity as it arises.

Vince is not <u>inefficient</u>, he just listens to his gut
                5
rather than being sucked into the games of Hollywood. In another episode, he turns down a movie
deal that he did not really want in hopes of getting
a <u>long-shot</u> deal. He does this because waiting
      6
for the long shot felt energizing and right and gave
him a huge <u>trickle</u> of excitement, whereas taking
              7
the sure-thing movie felt wrong.

1. (A) NO CHANGE
   (B) teaches
   (C) portrays
   (D) proves

2. (A) NO CHANGE
   (B) competition
   (C) trials
   (D) disputing

3. (A) NO CHANGE
   (B) agreed to
   (C) scheduled to
   (D) apparently to

4. (A) NO CHANGE
   (B) much a number of
   (C) many
   (D) fully many

5. (A) NO CHANGE
   (B) indifferent
   (C) absent
   (D) caring

6. (A) NO CHANGE
   (B) lengthy-shot
   (C) full of unsureness
   (D) elongated shot

7. (A) NO CHANGE
   (B) tweak
   (C) reaction
   (D) surge

Flow

Flow questions test you on the flow of an essay. They ask about the logical progression and organization of ideas in the essay, including questions about the introductory paragraph, body paragraphs, transition sentences, concluding paragraph, order of sentences, and order of paragraphs. In a Flow question that asks you to decide where to place a sentence, there is often a pronoun in the sentence, and you just need to find the sentence in the paragraph that the pronoun refers to. That's often the best way to find the right spot for the underlined sentence.

Here's the question from the Pretest.

I tried to will myself toward the glass doors. <u>"Now," I thought</u>. But I couldn't. Freedom was just twenty quick steps away, but I couldn't do it. ²⁹

29. If the writer were to delete the underlined sentence, the paragraph would lose

    (A) an important detail.
    (B) a transition from one sentence to the next.
    (C) some of its personal tone.
    (D) nothing at all, since this sentence is out of place.

Solution: Read the sentences before and after the underlined portion. Then use the process of elimination on the choices:

(A) ~~an important detail~~—Nope, it's not an important detail.
(B) ~~a transition from one sentence to the next~~—No, it does not make a transition from one thing to another.
(C) some of its personal tone—Yes, he tells the reader his thoughts; very personal.
(D) ~~nothing at all, since this sentence is out of place~~—Nope, the underlined sentence is not out of place. It fits into the flow of the paragraph very well.

Correct answer: C

SAT Mantra #29

For "flow" questions, use the process of elimination. In a Flow question that asks you to decide where to place a sentence, there is often a pronoun in the sentence, and you just need to find the sentence in the paragraph that the pronoun refers to.

Flow Drills

Every July, my family spends a few weeks on a "clothing-optional" beach on Martha's Vineyard. **1**
This section of Lucy Vincent Beach is the final stop on a half-mile stretch of sand, and it's the place my family has been planting their multi-colored beach umbrellas since the 1970s. **2**

As a little kid, I played happily, unconcerned about the nudity. My attitude toward the nude beach changed when I was twelve. Nothing around me made me feel that going to a nude beach was anything other than weird, and I abandoned my family's beach community. I kept away for three
                                    3
years, but the summer when I was fifteen, on the third day of our vacation (I still do not remember how it happened), it just felt right to get up and start walking down to the far end of the beach. Everyone loves the beach Fifty yards before my
            4
family's rainbow-colored beach umbrella, I ran to my "clothing-optional" family.

1 Which choice would best tie the introduction of this essay to the essay's concluding sentence?

Ⓐ NO CHANGE

Ⓑ special beach

Ⓒ the Lucy Vincent Beach

Ⓓ multi-colored beach umbrellas

2 At this point, the writer is considering adding the following true statement: The 1970s saw an oil crisis and the growth of the environmental movement. Should the writer make the addition here?

Ⓐ Yes, because the sentence provides more information about the 1970s.

Ⓑ Yes, because the sentence provides important background information about the author.

Ⓒ No, because the sentence is not supported by evidence to back it up.

Ⓓ No, because the sentence distracts from the paragraph's focus.

3 Ⓐ NO CHANGE

Ⓑ (Begin new paragraph) In keeping away

Ⓒ (Begin new paragraph) I kept away

Ⓓ (Do NOT begin new paragraph) In keeping away

4 Ⓐ NO CHANGE

Ⓑ Most people love the beach.

Ⓒ Everyone's love is the beach.

Ⓓ DELETE the underlined portion.

Goal Questions

Several questions on each test ask you to decide which answer choice would best accomplish a certain goal. I have seen this type of question boggle students. Usually, all the choices sound pretty good. **The key to this type of question is to choose the one choice that achieves the very specific goal stated in the question.** All the answers may sound pretty good, but only one of them will actually achieve the **goal**. Let's take a look at this on the Pretest. Once you know you are looking for the one choice that meets the specific goal stated in the question, these questions are easy!

Let's take a look at the goal question on the Pretest.

I turned and walked back down the hall.
                                   30

30. The writer wishes to add details that emphasize his trip back to his filing. Which statement would best accomplish this?

   (A) hall, down the harsh metal stairs, straight to the Filing Room, then to my filing.
   (B) hall, feeling the approval of my family.
   (C) hall, knowing that one day I would do more than just file.
   (D) hall, once again angry, yet perhaps more humble.

Solution: The specific goal for the question is to "add details that emphasize the writer's trip back to his filing." Choice A adds details about his walk back, and choices B, C, and D do not. They are interesting, and they refer to details in the essay, but they do not meet the **goal** that is specifically stated in the question. I love this strategy; once you know that you need to look for the goal, these questions are easy!

Correct answer: A

> SAT Mantra #30
> For "goal" questions, choose the one answer choice that achieves the
> very specific GOAL stated in the question.

Goal Questions Drills

Frederick Douglass was born on February 14, 1818. **1** This "Sage of Anacostia" is one of the most influential figures in African-American history. He was an ardent activist and a reformer of human rights.

Douglass was born into slavery. In 1838, at the age of 20, he successfully escaped his Maryland plantation and settled in Massachusetts. There he told his story and became a respected anti-slavery lecturer.

Douglass's most famous written work is his autobiography, *Narrative of the Life of Frederick Douglass, an American Slave*. **2** The book's vivid account informed the public and fueled the anti-slavery movement.

Douglass went on to publish several newspapers, including the *North Star*, whose motto was "Right is of no Sex—Truth is of no Color—God is the Father of us all, and we are all brethren." **3**

1 At this point, the writer wants to add a sentence that links the first two sentences. Assuming that all are true, which of the following would best accomplish this?

Ⓐ Doing some of his most influential work from his home in Anacostia, Washington, DC.

Ⓑ Born a slave, he wound up a revered reformer.

Ⓒ Because he lived for the last 20 years of his life in Anacostia, Washington, DC, he is associated with and often nicknamed for that place.

Ⓓ The exact date of his birth is not known.

2 In this paragraph, the writer intends to briefly describe the content of the autobiography. Which one of the following best accomplishes the writer's intention?

Ⓐ He went on to revise and republish the autobiography two times.

Ⓑ The book details Douglass's life from birth to escape from slavery.

Ⓒ The book received positive reviews and became an immediate best-seller.

Ⓓ Critics doubted its authenticity, skeptical of such eloquent language from someone who had not received a formal education.

3 Which of the following true statements, if inserted here, would best conclude the essay as well as maintain the tone established in the introduction?

Ⓐ Douglass also published *The New National Era*.

Ⓑ These publications affected many readers and helped advance the anti-slavery movement.

Ⓒ This "Sage of Anacostia" overcame great obstacles to become one of the most important reformers in U.S. history.

Ⓓ And, truly, Douglass lived this motto.

Yes or No?

Several questions on each test ask you to decide whether a passage accomplished a certain intention. This is a great opportunity for the process of elimination. Decide whether it did or did not, and then decide which reason is most correct. Every SAT has several of these questions, and many kids consider them the hardest type. But when you are used to the language, they are easy!

Did you catch this question on the Pretest?

31. Suppose the writer had been assigned to write a brief essay about internship opportunities in Bermuda. Would this essay fulfill the assignment?

(A) Yes, because the essay describes his reaction to his assignment.
(B) Yes, because the essay indicates the effect of internships on young people in Bermuda.
(C) No, because the essay restricts its focus to the writer's internship experience.
(D) No, because the essay does not describe how the writer learned from his internship.

Solution: Would the essay fulfill an assignment about internship opportunities in Bermuda? It did mention an internship in Bermuda, but only one. It was not about various opportunities, just about Kyle's one internship. It was a great essay, but it was not about internship opportunities.

Once you know that the answer is no, decide which reason is better. Choice C is perfect; the essay did not fulfill the assignment because it restricted its focus to the writer's internship. Choice D is incorrect because the writer did describe what he learned from his internship, but that does not matter to the assignment. Make sure that the answer you choose meets the whole assignment (all the words), not just the first part of it.

Correct answer: C

SAT Mantra #31
For a "yes/no"
question, choose an answer that applies to the entire question,
not just a few words of it.

Yes or No Drills

Many actors devote themselves entirely to studying Shakespeare, and there are schools explicitly for this purpose. These schools work to produce Shakespearean actors. But, ironically,
5 we do not know what training an actor actually received in Shakespeare's time.

The truth is that very little is known about the techniques used to train Shakespearean actors. We do not know the curriculum used. Nor do
10 we know the duration of training.

We do know that Shakespeare's plays include sword fights, brawls, dances, and music. We therefore conclude that actors needed to be familiar with and were trained in swordplay,
15 stage combat, dancing, and music.

The theater even incorporated realistic bloodshed. For example, sheep's or pig's organs were used in murder scenes, and sheep's blood was slashed about on swords and wounds.

1 Suppose the writer had decided to write an essay that summarizes the curriculum at the top three schools for studying Shakespearean acting. Would this essay fulfill the writer's goal?

(A) Yes, because the essay describes the training required of Shakespearean actors.

(B) Yes, because the essay includes the techniques and courses that these schools teach.

(C) No, because the essay argues that we know almost nothing about the training of Shakespearean actors.

(D) No, because the essay limits its focus to a general overview and does not go over the training at the top three schools.

2 The writer is considering deleting the phrase "The truth is that" from the first sentence of the second paragraph. If the writer were to delete this phrase, would the meaning of the sentence change?

(A) Yes, because the reader might doubt the validity of the assertion.

(B) Yes, because the sentence would become much weaker.

(C) No, because the phrase is an example of wordiness and is not needed in the sentence.

(D) No, because the following paragraph disproves the statement anyway.

3 Suppose the author had intended for the final paragraph to serve as a conclusion for the essay. Would the paragraph fulfill this goal?

(A) Yes, because the reader learns new information about stage combat.

(B) Yes, because the paragraph is full of powerful details.

(C) No, because the paragraph does not wrap up the essay as a whole.

(D) No, because the paragraph lacks sufficient details to back up its claim.

Adverbs End in "ly"

Read the following message:

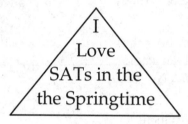

I
Love
SATs in the
the Springtime

What did it say?

"I Love SATs in the Springtime"? Yes, we do love SATs, and they're so great in the springtime. But that's not what it said. Read it again.

Did you catch it? It says, "I love SATs in **the the** springtime."

Cheap, right? But this is perfect practice for what the SAT does with "ly."

Sometimes, it leaves off the "ly" on an adverb, and you need to catch it. That's almost impossible if you're not watching for it, but easy if you are! Nasty, tricky SAT makers, but we know about and expect their tricks, so we get the questions right!

Did you catch it on the Pretest?

32. Now I worked <u>content</u>, happy to be learning.
     32

    (A) NO CHANGE
    (B) contentedly
    (C) in content
    (D) with contentedly

Solution: Kyle worked "contentedly," not "content." This is easy to catch if you know to watch for it. I'm not sure why the SAT has chosen to test this, but we know to watch for it, so these questions are easy points!

Correct answer: B

SAT Reading/Writing Mantra #32
Make sure to read the sentence as it really is.
Don't correct it in your head; i.e., watch for a missing "ly."

Adverbs End in "ly" Drills

Let's practice a few specific examples.

1 If I am understanding this article <u>correct, it is saying</u> that we should all be kind to one another.

    Ⓐ NO CHANGE

    Ⓑ correct, it says

    Ⓒ correctly; it says

    Ⓓ correctly, it is saying

2 The large green trucks that pass <u>constant through Paris</u> immaculately clean everything in sight.

    Ⓐ NO CHANGE

    Ⓑ constant in Paris

    Ⓒ constant through Paris'

    Ⓓ constantly through Paris

3 In this town I had avoided taking buses, which, due to the overall disorganization of the place, <u>brought me places more slow than my feet.</u>

    Ⓐ NO CHANGE

    Ⓑ brought me places that were more slow than my feet

    Ⓒ brought me places more slow than my feet would bring me

    Ⓓ brought me places more slowly than my feet

4 The place was <u>crowded, and I quickly</u> became separated from my friends in the attempt to advance toward a table.

    Ⓐ NO CHANGE

    Ⓑ crowded, and I quick

    Ⓒ crowded, and I was quick to be

    Ⓓ crowded; and I quickly

5 Sometimes hand gestures, miming, and charades are involved <u>when a tourist tries desperate to communicate</u> in order to find a bank, restaurant, or bathroom.

    Ⓐ NO CHANGE

    Ⓑ when a tourist tries to communicate desperately

    Ⓒ for a tourist to try desperately to communicate

    Ⓓ when a tourist tries desperately to communicate

6 A relationship between therapist and patient promotes <u>healing more quick</u> than when a patient is told how to feel and what to do.

    Ⓐ NO CHANGE

    Ⓑ a healing more quick

    Ⓒ healing more quickly

    Ⓓ healing that's more quicker

Jedi Master Yoda

"Named must your fear be before banish it you can."
Jedi Master Yoda

Great advice. True for Jedi training. True for the SAT. But unless you're an 800-year-old Jedi master, don't try speaking or writing in the passive voice; the SAT always favors the active voice. "Active voice" is just fancy grammar language for "be direct and to the point." This is actually part of Skills 34 and 35, but it comes up so much on the SAT that I wanted to give it its own section of drills. Look at these examples.

Active Voice	Passive Voice
I run.	Running is what I do.
Kumar ate a hamburger.	Eating a hamburger is what Kumar did.
The Hulk is incredible.	Incredible is what the Hulk is.

Let's see this on the Pretest.

From now on, <u>hard work I would do</u>.
33

33. (A) NO CHANGE
    (B) hard would be done by me
    (C) hard work is what I did
    (D) I would work hard.

Solution: "hard work I would do" uses the passive voice. You can hear it; it sounds weak, passive, indirect, and wordy. Choice D is in the active voice; it sounds much more powerful and direct. This is a great tool for your own writing. Writing in the active voice sounds more powerful and clear.

Correct answer: D

SAT Reading/Writing Mantra #33
On an SAT writing question, always choose the active over
the passive voice.

Jedi Master Yoda Drills

Here are a few examples for which practicing the active voice is something that you can do.

1 <u>Passing the CPA exam is what Juana did</u> last
    1
June, so now she practices accounting and can sign tax returns.

(A) NO CHANGE

(B) Of passing the CPA exam is something that Juana did

(C) What Juana did was pass the CPA exam

(D) Juana passed the CPA exam

2 <u>Indicating the time and effort the artist had put</u>
                    2
<u>into making it was the intention behind the high</u>
                    2
<u>price of the painting.</u>
        2

(A) NO CHANGE

(B) To indicate the time and effort the artist had put into making it was the intention behind the high price of the painting.

(C) The painting's high price was intended to indicate the time and effort the artist had put into making it.

(D) Intending to indicate the time and effort the artist had put into making the painting was the reason for the high price of the painting.

3 <u>Learning to cope with stress more effectively is</u>
                                    3
<u>the reason that many teenagers have started</u>
                    3
<u>practicing yoga.</u>
        3

(A) NO CHANGE

(B) Many teenagers have started practicing yoga to learn to cope with stress more effectively.

(C) Starting to practice yoga is what many teenagers have started doing; their reason being to learn to cope more effectively with stress.

(D) Learning to cope with stress is the more effective reason why many teenagers have started practicing yoga.

4 In *Monty Python and the Holy Grail,* <u>before King</u>
                                            4
<u>Arthur lobbed the Holy Hand Grenade of</u>
                4
<u>Antioch, five is the number he counted to.</u>
                            4

(A) NO CHANGE

(B) after counting to five, King Arthur then did the lobbing of the Holy Hand Grenade of Antioch.

(C) five being the number he counted to, he then lobbed the Holy Hand Grenade of Antioch.

(D) King Arthur counted to five before he lobbed the Holy Hand Grenade of Antioch.

Combining Sentences

Often the SAT asks you to do something. It is to combine two sentences. In fact, you know what, let's practice this wonderful skill by combining the first two sentences of this paragraph to "Often the SAT asks you to combine two sentences." Ahh, now, that sounds better. This is another way of being clear, direct, and nonredundant (Skill 26), as well as using the active voice (Skill 33). Make sure that if there is a transition word (skill 18), it is used appropriately, and make sure that a comma or semicolon is used correctly (Skill 22).

Let's review the question from the Pretest.

34. Which of the following is the best way to revise and combine the sentences reproduced below?

It turned out I didn't know everything. I knew barely anything of Bermuda's government.

(A) NO CHANGE
(B) It turned out I didn't know everything, I knew barely anything of Bermuda's government.
(C) It turned out I didn't know everything, in fact, I knew barely anything of Bermuda's government.
(D) It turned out I didn't know everything; and knew barely anything of Bermuda's government.

Solution: You can see that this is simply a combination of several Skills. The reproduced sentences are not too bad, but the question asks us to combine them. That makes sense, since the SAT loves conciseness. To find the correct answer, use the process of elimination. You know from Skill 22 that choice B would require a semicolon, since both parts of the sentence could stand alone. And you know from Skill 21 that choice D needs a comma instead of a semicolon, since the parts of the sentence could not stand alone. Choice C is best. It is clear and direct.

Correct answer: C

SAT Reading/Writing Mantra #34
For "combining sentences" questions, use the process of elimination to choose the answer that is the most clear and nonredundant.

Combining Sentences Drills

First let's practice combining sentences with the following example.

1 Which of the following is the best way to revise and combine the sentences reproduced below?

Professor Chen is a great instructor. He is known for his lucid explanations of even the most complex topics.

(A) Being a great instructor; lucid explanations for even the most complex topics are what Professor Chen is known for.

(B) A great instructor, Professor Chen is known for his lucid explanations of even the most complex topics.

(C) As being a great instructor, Professor Chen is known for his lucid explanations of even the most complex topics.

(D) Professor Chen is known for his lucid explanations of even the most complex topics, he is known to be a great instructor.

And now let's practice with the short passage below.

(1) Among all the books I've read, one of my favorites is the Harry Potter series. (2) There are seven books in that series. (3) I have three favorites. (4) This report is on Book One.

(5) For starters let's take a look at the Dursleys. (6) The Dursleys are normal, extremely normal, in fact their own brave but failing crusade to be utterly, fully, completely normal alienated them from those around them, consequently getting them more looks, stares, and whisperings-behind-backs than they would have gotten if they hadn't tried so hard.

(7) A truly remarkable boy with messy black hair, green eyes and a lightning-shaped scar on his forehead and, as far as the Durselys are concerned, a slug. (8) Harry is known as "the boy who lived" because he survived a dark curse cast by the evil Lord Voldemort. (9) His parents were killed and their house was destroyed, but Harry, a baby, survived.

(10) No one knows how Harry did it, how could a baby survive the same curse that killed so many powerful wizards far more powerful than Harry? (11) Very little is known, and that that is known is not known at all; it is only guesswork.

2 In context, which of the following is the best way to revise and combine sentences 2 and 3 (reproduced below)?

There are seven books in that series. I have three favorites.

(A) I have three favorites of the seven-book series.

(B) Seven books in the series, I have three that are favorites.

(C) Three favorites I have and there are seven total in the series.

(D) Of the seven books in the series, I have three favorites.

Skills Review:

3 Which of the following, if inserted before sentence 5, would make a good transition from the first paragraph?

(A) The book has many interesting characters.

(B) Where to start?

(C) Book Seven was good, too.

(D) Harry Potter is a fascinating character.

4 Which of the following sentences, if inserted before sentence 7, would best improve the third paragraph?

(A) So, that's the Dursleys.

(B) Why not be normal?

(C) Next, there's Harry Potter.

(D) How did Harry survive?

5 Which of the following would be most effective as a concluding sentence for the essay?

(A) Such intriguing story lines make *Harry Potter* such a fun series!

(B) The Dursleys and Harry Potter.

(C) So, we keep guessing.

(D) And that's Book One!

How to Think Like a Grammar Genius

You've now learned all the Skills that you need for the SAT writing multiple-choice questions. The Mantras remind you of what to do and when to do it. Let's make sure you've memorized and integrated the Mantras. Drill them until you are ready to teach them. Then do that.

Learning Mantras is like learning martial arts. Practice them until they become part of you, until you can follow them naturally: when you see an underlined verb, you look for its subject; when you see an underlined transition word or preposition, you ask if it fits; when you see an underlined pronoun, you check for clarity and agreement; you watch for "ly" on adverbs; you train and trust your ear; and you use the process of elimination. This will raise your SAT Writing score dramatically, and it will improve your actual writing too.

Check the box next to each Skill when you have mastered it. Reread the Skill sections if you need to.

☐ **Intro.** When something trips up your tongue or you can't get its meaning, it's probably wrong.

☐ **Skill 15.** When a verb is underlined, trust your ear. When in doubt, identify its subject and make sure that the singular/plural and tense match the subject.

☐ **Skill 16.** When a verb is underlined, identify the subject and cross out any prepositional phrases; a prepositional phrase NEVER counts as the subject of the verb. Also, ask what is doing the action of the verb, and watch for the second trick, where the subject comes after the verb.

☐ **Skill 17.** When a pronoun is underlined, we must be totally sure what noun it is referring to. If this is unclear in any way, the pronoun is incorrect. The underlined pronoun must also match (singular or plural) the noun that it refers to.

☐ **Skill 18.** When a transition word (such as "although," "since," "but," "therefore," or "however") is underlined, see whether it works in the sentence.

☐ **Skill 19.** When words in a list are underlined, make sure they match.

☐ **Skill 20.** When words being compared are underlined, make sure they match.

☐ **Skill 21.** When a comma is underlined, ask yourself, Should there be a pause here? Read it with and without a pause and see which works. Commas (and pauses) are used to set off a side note.

☐ **Skill 22.** Phrases that can stand alone are separated with a semicolon, a comma with "and," or a period.

☐ **Skill 23.** When a preposition is underlined, ask yourself if it is the right preposition to use.

☐ **Skill 24.** If "I" or "me" is underlined, test it by putting the I/me first or drop the other person and trust your ear. If "its" or "it's" is underlined, remember that "it's" means "it is" and "its" is possessive, like "that tree is nice; I like <u>its</u> colorful leaves."

☐ **Skill 25.** "My uncle's books" means that one uncle has books, and "my uncles' books" means that two or more uncles have the books. "-Er" or "more" is used to compare two things, and "-est" or "most' is used to compare more than two things. "Who" is for people, and "which" is for things. Watch for pairs of words such as "not only . . . but also" and "either . . . or."

☐ **Skill 26.** The SAT likes things crisp and clear; we always want the answer that is most clear, concise, direct, and nonredundant.

☐ **Skill 27.** A descriptive phrase on the SAT must be clearly associated with (and usually placed right next to) the noun described.

☐ **Skill 28.** Make sure that the underlined word fits into the context of the sentence.

☐ **Skill 29.** For "flow" questions, use the process of elimination. In a Flow question that asks you to decide where to place a sentence, there is often a pronoun in the sentence, and you just need to find the sentence in the paragraph that the pronoun refers to.

☐ **Skill 30.** For "goal" questions, choose the one answer choice that achieves the very specific **goal** stated in the question.

☐ **Skill 31.** For a "yes/no" question, choose an answer that applies to the entire question, not just a few words. of it.

☐ **Skill 32.** Make sure to read the sentence as it is. Don't correct it in your head; that is, watch for a missing "ly."

☐ **Skill 33.** On an SAT writing question, always choose the active over the passive voice.

☐ **Skill 34. For** "combining-sentences" questions, use the process of elimination to choose the answer that is the most clear and nonredundant.

> Let's apply these on the question from the Pretest.
>
> All I had known of local politics to that point had been gleaned from my parents' political banter, <u>lopsided as it was</u>.
>   34
>
> **35.** (A) NO CHANGE
>   (B) lopsided
>   (C) lopsided as the banter was being
>   (D) lopsided as it's

Solution: The underlined phrase sounds pretty good. Let's try the choices in case there is an even better option. Choice B makes no sense in the sentence. Choice C is too wordy, and "was being' sounds terrible. Choice D is incorrect, since "it's" means "it is," which sounds wrong and does not match the past tense of the rest of the sentence. So choice A is correct.

Let's apply the Mantras to see why: the pronoun "it" clearly refers to "banter," the comma correctly represents a pause, "was" matches the tense of the rest of the sentence, and the underlined clause is right next to "banter," which it describes. You don't need to do all that, though. You can just use the process of elimination and say, "The underlined words sound good, and the answer choices sound awful, so NO CHANGE."

Correct answer: A

How to Think Like a Grammar Genius Drills

In a <u>famous well known scene</u> in the movie *Jerry*
1

Maguire, one character tells another that he loves her and that she completes him. These concepts of love, completing someone, and even marriage have meant different things at different times <u>of history</u> .
2

Only recently have people married for love alone. Originally, people married for survival—they <u>live in tribes and depend</u> on each other for safety,
3

food, and shelter.

In the last 100 years, as the Industrial Revolution has made life for some <u>easier</u> the idea of marriage
4

for love has come about. <u>Its</u> now frowned upon in
5

some cultures to marry for financial and social gain.

People hope to marry the person <u>who</u> com-
6

pletes them, cares for them, likes them, and <u>stands by them; the person</u> that makes them feel at
7

ease. Before people married for need, and now they marry for need of love.

1. (A) NO CHANGE
   (B) famous, well-known scene,
   (C) famous scene
   (D) famous and well-known scene

2. (A) NO CHANGE
   (B) to history
   (C) in history
   (D) historically speaking

3. (A) NO CHANGE
   (B) were living and depending in tribes
   (C) live in tribes and are depending
   (D) lived in tribes and depended

4. (A) NO CHANGE
   (B) easier,
   (C) easier;
   (D) easier, and

5. (A) NO CHANGE
   (B) It's
   (C) It was
   (D) Presently, it is

6. (A) NO CHANGE
   (B) whom
   (C) whose
   (D) which

7. (A) NO CHANGE
   (B) stands by them. The person
   (C) stands by them—the person
   (D) stands by them the person

Essay

The SAT essay seems to be a mystery to many kids, but it turns out that the graders are trained to look for very specific elements. If you give the graders those elements, you'll ace the essay. In the next 14 Skills, I'll show you exactly what they are looking for.

The essay section is not testing to see if you are the next William Faulkner. It's not looking for creativity, and you won't be asked to cite Shakespeare. The essay is testing your ability to read a passage and analyze how the author went about making his or her point—something that you've probably done quite a bit in English or history class.

Your essay is graded by two readers, each of whom gives you a score of from 1 to 4 (yielding a total essay score of from 2 to 8) in each of three graded categories:

Reading (how well you demonstrate your understanding of the passage)

Analysis (how well you analyze the author's use of evidence, reasoning, and/or style)

Writing (the clarity and effectiveness of your writing)

As I mentioned, we know exactly what the essay graders are looking for. Give them what they want and your score flies!

Okay, you're at the test center. The room smells like high school French fries and feet. You've taken the Reading, Language, and Math sections, and you're beginning to curse your advisor for suggesting that you stay for the optional essay. The proctor tells you to open your test booklet to the next section, the essay. What do you do?

(1) Open your booklet.

(2) Read the essay passage.

(3) As you read the passage, ask yourself, "Self, how does the author make her point?" What evidence does she cite? What reasoning does she provide? What stylistic devices does she use? As you read, hold your pencil, and whenever you find an example of one of these elements, circle it, underline it, or make a note in the margin. By the way, did you get nervous just now when I mentioned "stylistic devices"? Fret not; that term just refers to any way in which the author helped you, the reader, get interested in the essay. Did she make you curious, make you mad, or make you afraid? If so, make a note in the margin.

After you have read the passage, then what? I'll tell you. And this one thing will change your essay score dramatically. Ready for it? Here it is: Read it again. Yep, read it a second time. And again, of course, as you read it, hold your pencil and make notes when you come upon the author's use of evidence, reasoning, and stylistic devices.

Remember that you receive three scores for your essay and that the first one simply measures whether you understand the essay. Read it twice and you'll nail that score. Not only that, but a thorough understanding of what you've read will boost both of your other scores, too. "What about time?" you say. "There's no time to read this thing twice. I'll skim it, so that I have plenty of time to write." Bad idea. First of all, you get 50 minutes, which is lots of time. And second, when you've invested the time to really understand the passage, you'll know exactly what to write—it will flow right out of you, and all three of your scores will fly. Reading is actually the most important step in the essay section. How can you produce intelligent analysis or an organized essay if you don't understand the passage? I believe it was Napoleon who said, "The key to writing an effective SAT essay resides in carefully reading the passage." Or, wait, maybe that was Mrs. Wheaton, my ninth-grade English teacher.

SAT Reading/Writing Mantra #36
Read the passage twice. While you are reading,
hold your pencil and underline, circle, or make notes in the margin
when you see evidence, reasoning, and stylistic devices.

Reading Drills

Let's take this Skill out for a spin. Read the following passage. Hold your pencil and note any evidence, reasoning, and stylistic devices that appeal to you. Then do it again.

As you read the following passage, consider how Martin Luther King, Jr. uses

1. Evidence, such as facts or examples, to support his claims.
2. Reasoning to develop his ideas and to connect claims and evidence.
3. Stylistic or persuasive elements, such as word choice or appeals to emotion, to add power to the ideas being expressed.

Adapted from Martin Luther King, Jr., "Beyond Vietnam—A Time to Break Silence." The speech was delivered at Riverside Church in New York City on April 4, 1967.

(1) Since I am a preacher by calling, I suppose it is not surprising that I have . . . major reasons for bringing Vietnam into the field of my moral vision. There is at the outset a very obvious and almost facile connection between the war in Vietnam and the struggle I, and others, have been waging in America. A few years ago there was a shining moment in that struggle. It seemed as if there was a real promise of hope for the poor—both black and white—through the poverty program. There were experiments, hopes, new beginnings. Then came the buildup in Vietnam, and I watched this program broken and eviscerated, as if it were some idle political plaything of a society gone mad on war, and I knew that America would never invest the necessary funds or energies in rehabilitation of its poor so long as adventures like Vietnam continued to draw men and skills and money like some demonic destructive suction tube. So, I was increasingly compelled to see the war as an enemy of the poor and to attack it as such.

(2) Perhaps a more tragic recognition of reality took place when it became clear to me that the war was doing far more than devastating the hopes of the poor at home. It was sending their sons and their brothers and their husbands to fight and to die in extraordinarily high proportions relative to the rest of the population. We were taking the black young men who had been crippled by our society and sending them eight thousand miles away to guarantee liberties in Southeast Asia which they had not found in southwest Georgia and East Harlem. And so we have been repeatedly faced with the cruel irony of watching Negro and white boys on TV screens as they kill and die together for a nation that has been unable to seat them together in the same schools. And so we watch them in brutal solidarity burning the huts of a poor village, but we realize that they would hardly live on the same block in Chicago. I could not be silent in the face of such cruel manipulation of the poor.

(3) My [next] reason moves to an even deeper level of awareness, for it grows out of my experience in the ghettoes of the North over the last three years—especially the last three summers. As I have walked among the desperate, rejected, and angry young men, I have told them that Molotov cocktails and rifles would not solve their problems. I have tried to offer them my deepest compassion while maintaining my conviction that social change comes most meaningfully through nonviolent action. But they ask—and rightly so—what about Vietnam? They ask if our own nation wasn't using massive doses of violence to solve its problems, to bring about the changes it wanted. Their questions hit home, and I knew that I could never again raise my voice against the violence of the oppressed in the ghettos without having first spoken clearly to the greatest purveyor of violence in the world today—my own government. For the sake of those boys, for the sake of this government, for the sake of the hundreds of thousands trembling under our violence, I cannot be silent.

(4) For those who ask the question, "Aren't you a civil rights leader?" and thereby mean to exclude me from the movement for peace, I have this further answer. In 1957 when a group of us formed the Southern Christian Leadership Conference, we chose as our motto: "To save the soul of America." We were convinced that we could not limit our vision to certain rights for black people, but instead affirmed the conviction that America would never be free or saved from itself until the descendants of its slaves were loosed completely from the shackles they still wear. . . . Now, it should be incandescently clear that no one who has any concern for the integrity and life of America today can ignore the present war. If America's soul becomes totally poisoned, part of the autopsy must read: Vietnam. It can never be saved so long as it destroys the deepest hopes of men the world over. So it is that those of us who are yet determined that America will be are led down the path of protest and dissent, working for the health of our land.

Essay Prompt

Write an essay in which you explain how Martin Luther King, Jr. builds an argument to persuade his audience that American involvement in the Vietnam War is unjust. In your essay, analyze how King uses one or more of the features listed in the box above (or features of your own choice) to strengthen the logic and persuasiveness of his argument. Be sure that your analysis focuses on the most relevant features of the passage.

Your essay should not explain whether you agree with King's claims, but rather explain how King builds an argument to persuade his audience.

Prove It!

The essay assignment asks you to consider how the author uses:

1. **Evidence**, such as facts or examples, to support his claims.
2. **Reasoning** to develop his ideas and to connect claims and evidence.
3. **Stylistic or persuasive elements**, such as word choice or appeals to emotion, to add power to the ideas being expressed.

What does each of these mean? We'll explore the first two in this Skill and the third in the Skill that follows.

The first item in the list, *evidence, such as facts or examples, to support his claims,* is pretty self-explanatory. The passage will include evidence to support the author's claim. You need to point out that evidence. You can write about the relevance of the evidence to the author's claims and how reliable the sources seem (for example, citing a study from Harvard Medical School might be more convincing than a quote from an episode of *SpongeBob*).

The second item, *reasoning to develop his ideas and to connect claims and evidence,* refers to the logic and the order of presentation in the passage. How does A lead to B and connect to C? Does the author build her argument in logical steps? Is the evidence woven into the argument effectively? Just mentioning a study from Harvard Medical School is not enough. Does the author demonstrate how the study supports her point?

Let's look at the essay assignment from the Pretest.

37. Write an essay in which you explain how the author builds an argument to persuade his audience that we need to save the beaches of Cape Cod. In your essay, analyze how the author uses one or more of the features listed in the box above (or features of your own choice) to strengthen the logic and persuasiveness of his argument. Be sure that your analysis focuses on the most relevant features of the passage.

Solution: Did your essay analyze the author's use of evidence? Did you assess the effectiveness of the author's reasoning? Is there more that you might have written?

SAT Reading/Writing Mantra #37
Think about the relevance and reliability of the author's evidence. Also consider the author's use of logical reasoning to connect that evidence to the argument. Does A lead to B and connect to C?

Prove It! Drills

Take another look at the passage in the Skill 36 Drills. Examine your notes in the margin. Answer the following questions. Is the author's evidence relevant to his argument? Is it powerful and compelling? Does it come from impressive, credible sources? Does the author smoothly link the evidence to his claims? What is the author's flow of reasoning? Does A lead to B and connect to C?

_____

_____

_____

_____

_____

_____

_____

_____

_____

_____

INSIDE TIP: *Credible* is a very impressive vocab word to use in your essay. Use it and you'll gain points.

Dude's Got Style

The third element of the assignment, *stylistic or persuasive elements, such as word choice or appeals to emotion, to add power to the ideas expressed*, might include the author making the reader feel afraid, sad, happy, or surprised. This might be achieved through using words to paint a picture of a scene that engages the reader, presenting a personal anecdote, asking rhetorical questions ("Know what I mean?"), or using certain loaded words (for example, using the words "endanger," "threaten," and "menace" to induce a scary tone). Are children in danger? Is something that we hold dear in need of protection?

We'll see lots of examples of this in the following skills.

Let's look at the pretest essay.

38. Write an essay in which you explain how the author builds an argument to persuade his audience that we need to save the beaches of Cape Cod. In your essay, analyze how the author uses one or more of the features listed in the box above (or features of your own choice) to strengthen the logic and persuasiveness of his argument. Be sure that your analysis focuses on the most relevant features of the passage.

Solution: Look back at the passage in the Pretest. Did the writer employ certain word choices, appeals to emotion, or other stylistic devices to add power to his argument? What did you write about? What else could you have mentioned?

SAT Reading/Writing Mantra #38
As you read the passage, watch for *stylistic or persuasive elements, such as word choice or appeals to emotion, to add power to the ideas expressed.*
This might include descriptive detail that engages the reader, presenting a personal anecdote, asking rhetorical questions, using certain loaded words, or inspiring emotion in the reader.

Dude's Got Style! Drills

Look again at the passage in the Skill 36 Drills. Examine your notes. Did the author call upon any stylistic devices to persuade the reader? Describe them here.

_____
_____
_____
_____
_____
_____
_____
_____
_____
_____
_____
_____
_____
_____
_____
_____
_____
_____
_____
_____
_____
_____
_____
_____
_____
_____
_____
_____
_____
_____

Craft Your Thesis

Okay, you've read the assignment; you've circled or underlined evidence, reasoning, and stylistic devices; and you've started to ignore the smell of French fries and feet in the cafeteria as well as the guy next to you chomping his gum. (This is why, when you do practice tests, you should hire a few people to tap pencils, chomp gum, and talk to themselves. Then you'll be truly prepared.)

So, now what? Do you decide whether you agree or disagree with the author? No. Your assignment is not to agree or disagree with him or her. Not at all. Your assignment is simply to analyze how the author made his or her point in the essay—to discuss the evidence the author cites, the reasoning the author uses, and any stylistic devices that the author employs to make her or his point.

So, what then? Should you make a long, extensive outline? That would be nice, but there really isn't enough time. And, anyway, you don't need one. You've circled or underlined references to evidence, reasoning, and stylistic devices; that's your outline. That is exactly what you'll write about. There's no time and no need to write a flowchart for your whole essay. Instead, take a look at the evidence, reasoning, and stylistic devices you have noted and craft your thesis statement. Your thesis is the blueprint for the essay.

Let's look at the essay assignment from the Pretest.

39. Write an essay in which you explain how the author builds an argument to persuade his audience that we need to save the beaches of Cape Cod. In your essay, analyze how the author uses one or more of the features listed in the box above (or features of your own choice) to strengthen the logic and persuasiveness of his argument. Be sure that your analysis focuses on the most relevant features of the passage.

Solution: Take a look at the evidence, analysis, and style elements that you've underlined or circled. What main elements are you going to discuss? The thesis cites the main idea that will be the focus of each body paragraph. Remember that you're not providing your opinion on the topic that the essay explores, you are analyzing the author's use of evidence, reasoning, and style. A student of mine, Tavi Wolfwood, wrote the following thesis for the Pretest essay: *Aza Lev builds his argument for the protection of Cape Cod's beaches by using personal anecdotes to engage the reader, questions and investigative style to lead the reader through the reasoning, and statistics and facts from reputable sources to support his point.* These examples form the outline for the body paragraphs of his essay—each the main idea of a paragraph.

SAT Reading/Writing Mantra #39
Look over the evidence, reasoning, and stylistic devices that you circled or underlined and craft your thesis. This is the outline for the body paragraphs of the essay.

Thesis Drills

Look again at the passage in the Skill 36 Drills. Examine your notes in the margin, and craft your thesis statement in the space below.

_____

_____

_____

_____

_____

_____

_____

_____

_____

_____

_____

_____

_____

_____

_____

_____

_____

_____

_____

_____

_____

_____

_____

Intro Paragraph

Your Intro

Your introductory paragraph should be short, maybe three to five sentences. Make the first sentence interesting if you can—a question, a quote, a surprising statement, or something clever. If you can't, that's okay; just ask or answer the question from the assignment. Then use a sentence or two to link that exciting statement or provocative question to your thesis. The thesis cites the specific examples that will be the focus of the body paragraphs. Remember that you're not providing your opinion on the topic, you are analyzing the author's use of evidence, reasoning, and style. Use the opener, link, and thesis as the format, and within that format, be yourself; let your style come through. Don't try to mimic someone else's style; let your own shine through.

> Let's apply this to the Pretest question.
>
> **40.** Write an essay in which you explain how the author builds an argument to persuade his audience that we need to save the beaches of Cape Cod. In your essay, analyze how the author uses one or more of the features listed in the box above (or features of your own choice) to strengthen the logic and persuasiveness of his argument. Be sure that your analysis focuses on the most relevant features of the passage.

Solution. Did the intro that you wrote provide the opening, link, and thesis?

Here's what Tavi wrote for his terrific essay:

> What's more relaxing than a summer trip to the beach? And how would you feel if we were in danger of losing these very beloved beaches? This is exactly what Aza Lev explores in *Cape Cod: The Threat to the Beauty*. Throughout the article, Lev develops his argument to persuade the audience of his opinion: that the beaches of Cape Cod need to be protected. Lev builds this argument by using personal anecdotes to engage the reader, questions and investigative style to lead the reader through his reasoning, and statistics and facts from reputable sources to support his point.

Tavi begins with an engaging hook—in this case, two questions that grab the reader. He then presents the issue and Aza Lev's stance on the issue, and follows up with his specific thesis statement. Remember that "opener, link, thesis" is a structure that you can play with. You can see that Tavi used this structure, but improvised. That's good. Use opener, link, and thesis as the format, and within that, be yourself. Don't try to mimic someone else's style; let your own shine through.

SAT Reading/Writing Mantra #40
Your intro paragraph should be 3 to 5 sentences: an opener, a link, and a thesis.

Write Your Intro Drills

Now that you have your details and your thesis planned, write your intro paragraph for your essay topic from the Skill 36 Drills. Use your opener, link, and thesis as the format, but within that, be yourself; let your style come through.

Transition Sentences

Each paragraph should start and end with a transition sentence of some kind. I'm not telling you to be totally boring and predictable. Just begin each new paragraph with a link to the previous one—a sentence that transitions/links the reader smoothly from one paragraph to the next—and make sure that each paragraph is tied up in some way. You can do this in a number of brilliant and creative ways.

Remember that each body paragraph should have a main focus. And that should allow for easy transitions from one to another. These transition sentences are also a great way to ensure that each paragraph stays focused. In fact, if coming up with a transition statement is very tough, perhaps that paragraph, or even your thesis, is too scattered or too general. Don't worry, we will practice this so that your paragraphs flow smoothly and are not scattered.

So, like I said, within this framework, make your transition statements your own, and make them brilliant. If you are not feeling brilliant and creative, you can just mention the previous paragraph and then introduce the main idea of the next, such as: "Now that you know that transition sentences are important, let's take a look at one that Tavi used to get a perfect score."

Once again, here's the question from the Pretest.

41. Write an essay in which you explain how the author builds an argument to persuade his audience that we need to save the beaches of Cape Cod. In your essay, analyze how the author uses one or more of the features listed in the box above (or features of your own choice) to strengthen the logic and persuasiveness of his argument. Be sure that your analysis focuses on the most relevant features of the passage.

Solution: Look at the transition sentences that you wrote. Do they introduce the main idea of each paragraph, link to the previous paragraph, and remind us of your thesis? It's not necessary for each one to fulfill all three of these goals, but each should nail at least one or two of them.

Here are a few nice transition sentences from Tavi's essay. You've seen his intro. Then he began his first paragraph with. "Lev sets his initial argument by presenting the reader with a personal anecdote." This made a nice transition from the intro to the first paragraph, which analyzes the anecdote. For the next paragraph, Tavi begins with, "The second stylistic element that Lev employs to demonstrate that the Cape Cod beaches are worth saving is the use of facts and statistics from well-known and influential sources." This is a great opener. It keeps the essay on track and reminds the reader of Tavi's thesis. To see these transition sentences in context, refer to his complete essay on page 149.

INSIDER ESSAY TIP #2: Use the word *employs,* as in "The second stylistic element that Lev employs. . . ." Graders dig it.

SAT Reading/Writing Mantra #41
Use transition sentences to begin each paragraph, link it to the previous paragraph, and/or remind the reader of your thesis.

Transition Sentences Drills

Okay, look back at the intro that you wrote in the Skill 39 Drills. The next paragraph or two explore the first element of your thesis. Your transition sentence should introduce the main idea of the paragraph, link to the previous paragraph, and/or remind the reader of your thesis.

Now let's see that transition sentence used to introduce the first body paragraph:

Body Paragraph I

Each "body" paragraph should be focused on a single main idea—a single specific topic such as the author's use of evidence, logical reasoning, or a call to emotion—with lots of details to back it up. That avoids the two biggest problems that I see in students' essays: lack of details and lack of focus. Organizing each paragraph around one topic automatically corrects both of these!

The highest-scoring essays that I have seen have used one of the following two designs for the body paragraphs. These are nice because they have organic organization and flow.

- One or two paragraphs to examine each of the topics listed in order in the thesis. (This is the style Tavi used in his essay about the Cape Cod beaches.)
- Analyze the passage in the order the material appears in the writing. In this case, your analysis is not grouped as Tavi's was (by topic), but analyzes each of the author's paragraphs as it develops and looks at what evidence, reasoning, and style the author employs as it shows up in order in the essay.

Let's look at what you did with your body paragraphs.

42. Write an essay in which you explain how the author builds an argument to persuade his audience that we need to save the beaches of Cape Cod. In your essay, analyze how the author uses one or more of the features listed in the box above (or features of your own choice) to strengthen the logic and persuasiveness of his argument. Be sure that your analysis focuses on the most relevant features of the passage.

Solution: Make sure that your body paragraphs are very detailed—the more details, the better. Usually, open with a transition sentence. You can remind the reader how this example demonstrates your thesis.

Here's what Tavi did for his first body paragraph:

> Lev sets his initial argument by presenting the reader with a personal anecdote, a photographic hook to appeal to the more emotional interests of the reader and engage him or her in the topic. As Lev begins his essay by allowing the reader to experience the beauty of the Cape Cod beaches, he causes the reader to feel an attachment to the place and therefore an investment in the topic. Beginning the essay in this way, before making the transition to the idea that "my children may never experience the serenity of this beach," is especially effective and allows Lev to hook the reader and evoke an emotional response. It allows Lev to more easily involve the reader in his cause: to save the Cape Cod beaches.

Tavi follows the order of his thesis. He writes around a single main idea—the author's use of a personal anecdote to hook his reader. Tavi especially gained points for pointing out the effectiveness of the author's flow: providing the engaging anecdote before mentioning the threat to this scene. Using details gets points, and so does pointing out the author's logical flow.

SAT Reading/Writing Mantra #42
Begin each "body" paragraph with a link to the previous paragraph, and write each around a single main idea.

Body Paragraph I Drills

You've already written the transition sentence. Now, let's see that first body paragraph.

Write an essay in which you explain how Martin Luther King, Jr. builds an argument to persuade his audience that American involvement in the Vietnam War is unjust. In your essay, analyze how King uses one or more of the features listed in the box above (or features of your own choice) to strengthen the logic and persuasiveness of his argument. Be sure that your analysis focuses on the most relevant features of the passage.

_____

_____

_____

_____

_____

_____

_____

_____

_____

_____

_____

_____

_____

_____

_____

_____

_____

_____

_____

_____

_____

_____

_____

Body Paragraph II

The next body paragraphs should develop the next point in your thesis. Like other body paragraphs, each of them should be organized around a specific main idea. Ideally, they should link smoothly to your previous body paragraph(s).

Let's see what you did.

43. Write an essay in which you explain how the author builds an argument to persuade his audience that we need to save the beaches of Cape Cod. In your essay, analyze how the author uses one or more of the features listed in the box above (or features of your own choice) to strengthen the logic and persuasiveness of his argument. Be sure that your analysis focuses on the most relevant features of the passage.

Solution: The paragraph that you wrote should revolve around one main idea, contain specific details, and reflect your thesis. Let's look at Tavi's essay:

An anecdote grabs a reader's attention, but Aza Lev knows that in order to inspire action, an anecdote must be followed up with reliable facts and figures. Lev cites facts and statistics from well-known and influential sources that convince the reader beyond a doubt that the Cape Cod beaches are both in need and worthy of saving. He presents statistics from the National Park Service and the Massachusetts Office of Coastal Zone Management such as "Over 450 species of amphibians, reptiles, fish, birds, and mammals, and a myriad of invertebrate animals" and "65%–70% of the coastline is eroding." These two federal organizations lend legitimacy and credibility to his presentation and ready him for the next phase of his argument for the protection of the Cape Cod beaches.

Tavi begins with a great transition linking this to the previous paragraph. He makes a generalization that he then backs up with two direct citations from the passage. This paragraph demonstrates his point that Lev uses compelling statistics from credible sources in order to win over the reader to his argument.

Notice that Tavi's essay is truly awesome, but not perfect. You cannot write a perfect essay in 50 minutes. The graders know this and allow for it. They call this allowance "holistic grading." They don't have a checklist, grade each item, and add up your points, like your English teacher might do for an essay where you have two weeks in which to do three drafts. Instead, they look at the essay as a whole and say, "Okay, he had good solid organization, a few spelling errors, but wow, he blew me away with details and depth. I'll give it a 4." If you give the graders what they want (structure, transitions, details, and analysis), you will get a high score. This makes the essay easy to ace.

SAT Reading/Writing Mantra #43
The next body paragraph(s) should address the second point in your thesis. It should be organized around a specific main idea. Ideally, it should link smoothly to your previous body paragraph(s).

Body Paragraph II Drills

Let's practice the next body paragraph(s) for our topic:

Write an essay in which you explain how Martin Luther King, Jr. builds an argument to persuade his audience that American involvement in the Vietnam War is unjust. In your essay, analyze how King uses one or more of the features listed in the box above (or features of your own choice) to strengthen the logic and persuasiveness of his argument. Be sure that your analysis focuses on the most relevant features of the passage.

_____

_____

_____

_____

_____

_____

_____

_____

_____

_____

_____

_____

_____

_____

_____

_____

_____

_____

_____

_____

_____

_____

_____

_____

A Strong Body

Your next body paragraph or two should develop the next aspect of your thesis. Again, begin with a transition, describe your point, back it up with powerful evidence from the passage, and wrap it up as you conclude the section and remind the reader of your thesis. And within this, feel free to go deep. Analyze with abandon. I like to call this *stretching the dough*. Imagine that you have a lump of pizza dough. Stretch it out. Make it bigger; that is, write more. Go deeper. Analyze more. Refer to additional evidence from the passage.

> **44.** Write an essay in which you explain how the author builds an argument to persuade his audience that we need to save the beaches of Cape Cod. In your essay, analyze how the author uses one or more of the features listed in the box above (or features of your own choice) to strengthen the logic and persuasiveness of his argument. Be sure that your analysis focuses on the most relevant features of the passage.

Solution: Tavi's third point in his thesis is that Lev uses rhetorical questions (stylistic questions that a writer or speaker poses without expecting an answer from the reader or listener).

Let's have a look:

> Lev skillfully brings the reader through his reasoning with the use of rhetorical questions throughout the article. He leads the reader through his argument with questions such as, "What is this long-term solution to preserve the beauty, wildlife, and culture of Cape Cod?" causing the reader to ponder the answer and become engaged and interested in the topic at hand. Later he asks, "What can you and I do to save these beaches, these cultural landmarks and wildlife refuges?" Lev even makes this question personal, addressing the reader directly. The questions draw the reader in, awakening him or her, as it were, to the topic as he or she reads the passage. We all know that discovering something for ourselves is far more powerful than simply being told it. Allowing the reader to answer questions and come to her or his own conclusions brings readers more deeply into Lev's cause.

Nice paragraph. Solid opening sentence. He clearly states his point, then backs it up with citations from the passage. Nice analysis, looking at the psychology of why Lev's rhetorical questions are effective.

SAT Reading/Writing Mantra #44
Support your generalizations with relevant paraphrases and quotations from the passage.

A Strong Body Drills

Let's see more of your body (paragraphs):

Write an essay in which you explain how Martin Luther King, Jr. builds an argument to persuade his audience that American involvement in the Vietnam War is unjust. In your essay, analyze how King uses one or more of the features listed in the box above (or features of your own choice) to strengthen the logic and persuasiveness of his argument. Be sure that your analysis focuses on the most relevant features of the passage.

_____

_____

_____

_____

_____

_____

_____

_____

_____

_____

_____

_____

_____

_____

_____

_____

_____

_____

_____

_____

_____

_____

_____

_____

What's the Problem?

It makes you look awfully smart when you point out something that the author might have done to make his or her argument even stronger. Most of your essay will analyze what the author did right in developing an argument. That's great, and it works because, let's face it, the SAT selects passages with well-developed and effective arguments. BUT, there's always something that might have been said better or differently.

Let's look at the Pretest.

45. Write an essay in which you explain how the author builds an argument to persuade his audience that we need to save the beaches of Cape Cod. In your essay, analyze how the author uses one or more of the features listed in the box above (or features of your own choice) to strengthen the logic and persuasiveness of his argument. Be sure that your analysis focuses on the most relevant features of the passage.

Solution: Did you include a paragraph on what might have been different? Tavi did not, which is fine. But here's an example of something that he could have included:

Aza Lev presents a solid and compelling argument for the need to save the beaches of Cape Cod. He leaves the reader informed, convinced, and ready to do his or her part to save these valuable natural landmarks. Yet, what might he have done differently to establish this point even more firmly? Lev could have provided more directions for the reader to take to make a difference and to help save the beaches. Lev has captured the reader's interest and converted him or her to his side of the argument, but the reader is left without knowing what do next. Lev would have made an even stronger case if he had concluded with a short list of organizations that the reader could contact or join to help save the beaches. Even better, he could have provided two or three very concrete steps that the reader could take to make a difference.

Good transition. Nice summary of the essay thus far. Great rhetorical question. Hey, why not show some style even here in your essay that analyzes style!

SAT Reading/Writing Mantra #45
If you have time, add a paragraph about what the author might have improved.

What's the Problem? Drills

Is there anything that even Martin Luther King, Jr. might have added to this effective and legendary speech?

_____

_____

_____

_____

_____

_____

_____

_____

_____

_____

_____

_____

_____

_____

_____

_____

_____

_____

_____

_____

_____

_____

_____

_____

_____

_____

_____

Stretch the Dough

The College Board has made one thing very clear: How much you write matters. Whenever it gives examples of essays with varying scores, each essay with a successively higher score is longer than the one before it. So if you want to maximize your score, write more. Not just filler, of course; you must write about things that matter, that demonstrate the skills we have looked at thus far. Writing more is easy. Just refer to another piece of evidence from the passage. Or explain more clearly how a citation from the passage was effective. Analyze more deeply. Go out on a limb. Remember how Tavi made the leap about the effective psychology of Lev's rhetorical questions. Expand more on whatever you just wrote. Explain your thinking more clearly. Speculate on why an author chose a certain logic or style. Whatever you are writing about, give additional evidence and additional analysis.

46. Write an essay in which you explain how the author builds an argument to persuade his audience that we need to save the beaches of Cape Cod. In your essay, analyze how the author uses one or more of the features listed in the box above (or features of your own choice) to strengthen the logic and persuasiveness of his argument. Be sure that your analysis focuses on the most relevant features of the passage.

Solution: Is your essay long enough? What could you have further developed? Where could you have explained yourself more clearly? Would additional evidence from the passage have been effective? Is there a spot where you could have gone deeper? What about an extra paragraph exploring what Lev could have done differently?

SAT Reading/Writing Mantra #46
Write more.

Stretch the Dough Drills

Let's practice stretching the dough.

Choose one of your body paragraphs and rewrite it below, adding more, more, more . . .

_____

_____

_____

_____

_____

_____

_____

_____

_____

_____

_____

_____

_____

_____

_____

_____

_____

_____

_____

_____

_____

_____

_____

_____

_____

Conclusion

Your conclusion should wrap up your essay. Generally it should follow this format: restate thesis, link, and end with a bang. The bang is like the opener. It can be a question, a quote, a surprising statement, the next step, an action that the reader can take, or something else clever.

Also—and this is very important—watch your pacing and leave time to write the conclusion. You might think that the graders would say, "Well, I know that this nice teenager had only 50 minutes, so I can see why she didn't include a conclusion" or something like that. But no, you lose points for leaving it out. Remember, the basic element that the graders are testing is organization. If there's no conclusion, they must assume that you didn't know you needed one. So when you have maybe 5 minutes left, close up the body paragraph and write the conclusion. Brilliant is good, but a conclusion of even a modest sentence or two will get you points.

> Let's see what you did with your conclusion.
>
> **47.** Write an essay in which you explain how the author builds an argument to persuade his audience that we need to save the beaches of Cape Cod. In your essay, analyze how the author uses one or more of the features listed in the box above (or features of your own choice) to strengthen the logic and persuasiveness of his argument. Be sure that your analysis focuses on the most relevant features of the passage.

Solution: The conclusion that you wrote should wrap up the essay. You can use the format restate thesis, link, and bang. Make sure you have proved your point.

Let's look at Tavi's conclusion.

> Personal anecdotes, statistics and facts from reputable sources, and rhetorical questions: all of these relevant features within the essay allow Aza Lev to build his argument for saving the beaches of Cape Cod. His personal anecdotes engage the reader, statistics and facts expand on the topic and present relevant data in order to convince the reader of the magnitude of the issue, and rhetorical questions allow Lev to bring the reader, personally engaged, through his argument in a step-by-step fashion, building his argument and convincing the reader of the necessity to save the Cape Cod beaches. After reading Aza Lev's "Cape Cod: The Threat to the Beauty," I'm ready to get up and do my part. Are you?

Nice conclusion. He restates his thesis, summarizes his main points, and ends with a nice bang. After writing about Lev's use of rhetorical questions and engaging the reader personally, he does this as well. Again, notice that Tavi's essay is not perfect. How can it be in 50 minutes? I mention this only to take the pressure off. Don't expect your essay to be perfect. No doubt with a few more hours, Tavi could clean it up. But it's very good, and, most important, it accomplishes what the SAT wants—the things that we know the graders give points for. It's organized, detailed, deep, and interesting, and that made for a great score!

INSIDER TIP: Use a colon correctly and you'll gain points.

SAT Reading/Writing Mantra #47
Structure your conclusion by restating your thesis, linking, and ending with a bang.

Conclusion Drills

Write a conclusion for your essay.

Other Stuff That Matters

You've got the format—intro, body paragraphs, and conclusion—you've quoted and paraphrased lots of specific evidence from the passage, and you have nice transition sentences. What else do you need? Remember that you get three grades for your essay: a grade for showing that you understood the passage, a grade for your analysis, and a grade for your writing. Here's a reminder of six things that add points to these scores. Add them, and I guarantee you'll gain points!

1 **Depth of analysis.** Don't be afraid to be deep—within the safe framework of intro, body paragraphs, and conclusion, go out on a limb: analyze things, make insights, state your observations, and draw conclusions.

2 **Length.** Longer is better; it makes you look eager and smart, and it gives you more opportunity to demonstrate that you understood the passage and to analyze the author's use of evidence, reasoning, and/or style. All else equal, longer essays score higher than shorter ones.

3 **Big words.** The SAT loves big vocab words, so use a bunch of them. (But make sure to use them correctly.) If this does not come easily to you, plan to have a few words that you will always use. We'll practice this in the drills. This is a guaranteed way to add points!

4 **Varied sentences.** Don't use all short, choppy sentences, and don't use all long, complex sentences. Use a variety. This makes an essay easier and more interesting to read. Variety keeps a reader awake and interested. And remember, use a colon or semicolon correctly and you'll gain points!

5 **Readable handwriting.** Technically, the graders don't grade for handwriting, but of course they do need to be able to read your essay. Try not to annoy them with handwriting that looks like the footprints left by a dying chicken. Do the best you can. Put a little extra effort into neatness. But don't overstress; I have seen some pretty bad handwriting get perfect scores! Bottom line: make it readable.

6 **Few or no grammar and spelling errors.** Make sure to proofread. Leave two or three minutes for proofing. More about this in Skill 49.

Back to the Pretest.

48. Write an essay in which you explain how the author builds an argument to persuade his audience that we need to save the beaches of Cape Cod. In your essay, analyze how the author uses one or more of the features listed in the box above (or features of your own choice) to strengthen the logic and persuasiveness of his argument. Be sure that your analysis focuses on the most relevant features of the passage.

Solution: In your essay, did you go deep, write 3 pages at the very least, use some impressive vocab, vary your sentences, write readably, and avoid basic grammar and spelling errors? Adding any one of these will earn you points.

You'll have a chance to practice elements in the Drills and in the remaining Skills.

SAT Reading/Writing Mantra #48
In your essay, go deep, write 3 pages at the very least, use some impressive vocab, vary your sentences, write readably, and avoid basic grammar and spelling errors.

Other Stuff That Matters Drills

How do you use more impressive vocabulary in your essay? I learned this strategy from a student who would plan several big words that he knew he would use. He got a perfect score every time. Obviously some words will be easier to use than others. "Ululation" (a howl) might be hard to work in, but "credibility" (believability), "inherent" (naturally occurring), or "incontrovertible" (unquestionable) could be used in **any** essay. For example, "Brian Leaf incontrovertibly demonstrates that the credibility of evidence is inherent in the success of any persuasive essay." Now you try. Below are a bunch of great essay words. Use these or choose a few of your own from English class, and try to incorporate them in the drill below. Then use them again in the practice essay for Skill 49.

1 Define each of the following great essay words:

Immutable_____   Concordant _____

Eradicated _____   Pertinent _____

Auspicious _____   Thwart _____

Superfluous _____   Ramification _____

Affinity _____

2 Let's practice incorporating these tips. In the space below, take one of the body paragraphs that you wrote for Skill 44 or 45 and rewrite it, incorporating more of the following: depth of insight, length, impressive vocab, sentence variety, neatness, and proofreading.

_____

_____

_____

_____

_____

_____

_____

_____

_____

_____

_____

_____

_____

_____

_____

_____

Proofread

"Write the first draft as a free write," Mrs. Schwartzonagel always said. "Don't worry about spelling and grammar; just get your ideas on paper." This was great advice, and I still use it. But for the SAT essay, it creates a mess. On the SAT, you need to attend to spelling and grammar as you write. Write quickly enough to capture your creative ideas as they come to you and quickly enough to finish in 50 minutes, but slowly enough to catch careless errors.

This is another one of those cool life skills. It's great to have the freedom and the flexibility to meet different demands with appropriate measures. Like when Big Sally gets up to bat and you say, "Back it up in the outfield!" For a long-term project, do a creative free-write. But when you are writing a 50-minute timed essay, attend to spelling and grammar as you go.

Then, when you have 5 minutes left, make sure you've written your conclusion and take a few minutes to proofread. This is not a complex reanalysis, just a basic reading over to find and correct big errors. This will definitely get you points.

Here's what you are looking for:

1. **Omitted words.** Because you are writing quickly, your hand may leave out a word that you meant to write. Example: Critics contend that the government overspends— superfluous items.
2. **Obvious misspellings.** There may be some words you're not sure of; do the best you can. But look for words that of course you know how to spell, but when you were writing furiously, you made a careless error.
3. **Obvious punctuation errors.** There may be some commas you're not sure of; do the best you can. Fix any obvious errors.
4. **Indenting.** Make sure you indented clearly.
5. **Paragraphs.** Make sure you started new paragraphs when you meant to.
6. **Details.** Make sure that you wrote what you meant to and not accidentally something else.

Back to the Pretest.

49. Write an essay in which you explain how the author builds an argument to persuade his audience that we need to save the beaches of Cape Cod. In your essay, analyze how the author uses one or more of the features listed in the box above (or features of your own choice) to strengthen the logic and persuasiveness of his argument. Be sure that your analysis focuses on the most relevant features of the passage.

Solution: Check over your Pretest essay or an essay from the Drills sections. Practice looking for and correcting the most common careless errors listed above.

SAT Reading/Writing Mantra #49
Leave a few minutes to proofread your essay for omitted words, misspellings, and punctuation errors, and to make sure that you have represented details accurately and started new paragraphs where you meant to by indenting.

Proofreading Drills

In the space below, practice writing a paragraph quickly, but still attending to spelling and grammar.

For this exercise, write a paragraph on any topic you like, but use at least four of the words "immutable," "concordant," "eradicated," "pertinent," "auspicious," "thwart," "superfluous," or "ramification."

_____

_____

_____

_____

_____

_____

_____

_____

_____

_____

_____

_____

_____

_____

_____

_____

_____

_____

_____

_____

Now, take a few minutes to proofread your paragraph for omitted words, misspellings, and punctuation errors, and to make sure that you have indented when you meant to and written details accurately. This is great practice, and it will definitely improve your score.

How to Be a Writing Monster

Review the Mantras below for our 14 essay Skills. Go back and reread the Skills for any that you feel unsure of. Then check the box next to each Skill when you believe you have mastered it.

☐ **Skill 36**. Read the passage twice. While you are reading, hold your pencil and underline, circle, or make notes in the margin when you see evidence, reasoning, and stylistic devices.

☐ **Skill 37**. Think about the relevance and reliability of the author's evidence. Also consider the author's use of logical reasoning to connect that evidence to the argument. Does A lead to B and connect to C?

☐ **Skill 38**. As you read the passage, watch for *stylistic or persuasive elements, such as word choice or appeals to emotion, to add power to the ideas expressed*. This might include descriptive detail that engages the reader, presenting a personal anecdote, asking rhetorical questions, using certain loaded words, or inspiring emotion in the reader.

☐ **Skill 39.** Look over the evidence, reasoning, and stylistic devices that you circled or underlined and craft your thesis. This is the outline for the body paragraphs of the essay.

☐ **Skill 40.** Your intro paragraph should be 3 to 5 sentences: an opener, a link, and a thesis.

☐ **Skill 41.** Use transition sentences to begin each paragraph, link it to the previous paragraph, and/or remind the reader of your thesis.

☐ **Skill 42.** Begin each "body" paragraph with a link to the previous paragraph, and write each around a single main idea.

☐ **Skill 43.** The next body paragraph(s) should address the second point in your thesis. It should be organized around a specific main idea. Ideally, it should link smoothly to your previous body paragraph(s).

☐ **Skill 44.** Support your generalizations with relevant paraphrases and quotations from the passage.

☐ **Skill 45.** If you have time, add a paragraph about what the author might have improved.

☐ **Skill 46.** Write more.

☐ **Skill 47.** Structure your conclusion by restating your thesis, linking, and ending with a bang.

☐ **Skill 48.** In your essay, go deep, write 3 pages at the very least, use some impressive vocab, vary your sentences, write readably, and avoid basic grammar and spelling errors.

☐ **Skill 49.** Leave a few minutes to proofread your essay for omitted words, misspellings, and punctuation errors, and to make sure that you have represented details accurately and started new paragraphs where you meant to by indenting.

That's it. You are ready to write a freakishly good essay. Let's go to the drills.

How to Be a Writing Monster Drills

List ten ways in which you could have improved your essay from the Pretest.

1. _____

_____

_____

2. _____

_____

3. _____

_____

4. _____

_____

5. _____

_____

6. _____

_____

7. _____

_____

8. _____

_____

9. _____

_____

10. _____

_____

Bonus Skill: Writing the Perfect SAT Essay

Life goes by pretty fast. If you don't stop and look around once in a while, you could miss it.
Ferris Bueller, *Ferris Bueller's Day Off* (Paramount Pictures, 1986)

Want the perfect essay? Here are the four steps to do it.

But first you have to promise me that you are doing this because you want to, and not out of some obsessive, sleep doesn't matter, gotta please my parents, if I don't go to Tufts I'm nothing misunderstanding. Strive to do well, yes. Also stay balanced. Sleep. Eat well. Exercise. Be true to yourself. Be brave. Be honest. Be relaxed. Breathe. And from that place, give it all you've got.

1. Make sure you understand all 15 essay writing Skills and all 21 writing multiple-choice Skills; this is the same grammar that they are looking for on the essay. Don't just look at them and say, "Yeah, I can do that." Practice. Do the drills. For the grammar Skills, make sure you can answer every question on every Skill correctly. If you can't, reread the section, reread the solutions, and keep redoing the drills until they make perfect sense. Then teach them to a friend.

2. Master Posttests I, II, and III (Posttests II and III are available online at www.MH-SAT-TOP50-Reading.com). Take each test, read the solutions, and redo any questions that you missed. When you have mastered these questions, your grammar is up to the task!

3. Then get a copy of *The Official SAT Study Guide,* published by the College Board. It contains four practice tests. Take all four timed practice essays. Use our essay Mantras to check each essay, and ask a friend, parent, or teacher to use the checklist on page 146. Practice pacing. Practice applying the Skills.

4. Writing an organized intro, body, conclusion essay will earn you a decent score. Proofreading, using transition sentences, citing lots of specific details from the passage, depth of analysis, and great vocab will boost you to perfect. Connecting your examples seems to be very important; it gives your essay cohesiveness and organically adds depth of analysis. Connecting examples can mean using the methods listed in Skills 43 and 44 and/or having a thread or theme running through the whole essay.

Let's see this all put into action in Tavi's essay. Notice again that this essay is not error-free, but it contains what graders are looking for. Also, don't be intimidated by this essay; I think that if an essay could get a score higher than all 4s, his would!

Tavi's Terrific Essay

Assignment: Write an essay in which you explain how the author builds an argument to persuade his audience that we need to save the beaches of Cape Cod. In your essay, analyze how the author uses one or more of the features listed in the box above (or features of your own choice) to strengthen the logic and persuasiveness of his argument. Be sure that your analysis focuses on the most relevant features of the passage.

What's more relaxing than a summer trip to the beach? And how would you feel if we were in danger of losing these very beloved beaches? This is exactly what Aza Lev explores in *Cape Cod: The Threat to the Beauty*. Throughout the article, Lev develops his argument to persuade the audience of his opinion: that the beaches of Cape Cod need to be protected. Lev builds this argument by using personal anecdotes to engage the reader, questions and investigative style to lead the reader through his reasoning, and statistics and facts from reputable sources to support his point.

Lev sets his initial argument by presenting the reader with a personal anecdote, a photographic hook to appeal to the more emotional interests of the reader and engage him or her in the topic. As Lev begins his essay by allowing the reader to experience the beauty of the Cape Cod beaches, he causes the reader to feel an attachment to the place and therefore an investment in the topic. Beginning the essay in this way, before making the transition to the idea that "my children may never experience the serenity of this beach," is especially effective and allows Lev to hook the reader and evoke an emotional response. It allows Lev to more easily involve the reader in his cause to save the Cape Cod beaches.

An anecdote grabs a reader's attention, but Aza Lev knows that in order to inspire action, an anecdote must be followed up with reliable facts and figures. Lev cites facts and statistics from well-known and influential sources that convince the reader beyond a doubt that the Cape Cod beaches are both in need and worthy of saving. He presents statistics from the National Park Service and the Massachusetts Office of Coastal Zone Management such as "Over 450 species of amphibians, reptiles, fish, birds, and mammals, and a myriad of invertebrate animals" and "65%–70% of the coastline is eroding." These two federal organizations lend legitimacy and credibility to his presentation and ready him for the next phase of his argument for the protection of the Cape Cod beaches.

Lev skillfully brings the reader through his reasoning with the use of rhetorical questions throughout the article. He leads the reader through his argument with questions such as "What is this long-term solution to preserve the beauty, wildlife and culture of Cape Cod?" causing the reader to ponder the answer and become engaged and interested in the topic at hand. Later he asks, "What can you and I do to save these beaches, these cultural landmarks and wildlife refuges?" Lev even makes this question personal, addressing the reader directly. The questions draw the reader in, waking him or her, as it were, to the topic as they read the passage. We all know that discovering something for ourselves is far more powerful than simply being told. Allowing the reader to answer questions and make their own conclusions brings them more deeply into Lev's cause.

Personal anecdotes, statistics and facts from reputable sources, and rhetorical questions: all of these relevant features within the essay allow Aza Lev to build his argument for saving the beaches of Cape Cod. His personal anecdotes engage the reader, statistics and facts expand on the topic and present relevant data in order to convince the reader of the magnitude of the issue, and rhetorical questions allow Lev to bring the reader, personally engaged, through his argument in a step by step fashion, building his argument and convincing the reader of the necessity to save the Cape Cod beaches. After reading Aza Lev's "Cape Cod: The Threat to the Beauty," I'm ready to get up and do my part. Are you?

This is the essay that we looked at in the essay Skills. Tavi demonstrated that he understood the passage; he analyzed evidence, reasoning, and style; and he gave the graders organization, vocabulary, details, connected examples, and amazing depth for a great score.

Easy, Medium, Hard, and Guessing Revisited

Let's revisit what I told you way back at the beginning of the book. It will probably make even more sense now.

The SAT is not graded like an English test at school. To get a 500, the average score for kids across the country, you need to get about half the questions correct. To get a 600, the average score for admission to schools like Goucher and the University of Vermont, you need about 75% correct. And for a beautiful 700 on the SAT, the average for kids who got into schools like Georgetown, U.C. Berkeley, Emory, and Wesleyan, you must answer 89% of the questions correctly.

Use this info to determine how many questions you need to answer correctly on the SAT. Knowing this is important because if you need only half or 70% of the answers correct, don't rush to get to every question. All questions are worth the same amount. Not rushing is the best way to avoid careless errors. In school, you might need to finish tests in order to do well. Here you do not. **You need to get to every question only if you are shooting for 700 or higher.**

Of course, since there is no penalty for wrong answers, you'll still bubble in an answer for every question, even ones that you don't have time to work through. And, best of all, now that you've completed this book, you know the Skills, you're prepared for the tricks, you'll be able to work faster and yet more accurately, and you'll barely need to guess. When you feel stumped, take another look and ask yourself, Which reading/writing Skill can I use?

Now What?

Take the Posttest. It contains questions that review our 50 Skills. Check your answers and review the Skills for any questions that were difficult. Then take the additional Posttests online at www.MH-SAT-TOP50-Reading.com. Again, check your answers and review the Skills for any questions that were difficult.

After you have completed the Posttests, go to your guidance office and pick up the free SAT packet, which contains a full practice test with answers and scoring instructions. Or you can download a free test at www.collegeboard.com.

Take the test as a dress rehearsal; get up early on a Saturday, time it, use the answer sheets, and fill in the ovals. If you have completed this book, you will find that you are very well prepared. Correct and score the test, and review whatever you got wrong. Figure out which Mantras you could have used to get those questions right.

If you have some time, purchase *The Official SAT Study Guide*, published by the College Board. It contains four practice tests. Take one practice test each week as a dress rehearsal. Take it when you are relaxed and focused. We want only your best work. Less than that will earn you a lower score than you are capable of and is bad for morale. Score each test and review whatever you got wrong. Figure out which Mantras you could have used to get those questions right.

Now, you are ready, you beautiful SAT monster. Go get 'em!

Posttest I

This Posttest contains questions that correspond to our 50 Skills. Take the test. Then check your answers and review the Skills for any questions that were difficult.

Each passage or pair of passages below is followed by a number of questions. After reading each passage or pair, choose the best answer to each question based on what is stated or implied in the passage or passages and in any accompanying graphics (such as a table or graph).

Note: This is a passage that you read earlier in Skill 9. Now, let's answer some questions about it.

The following passage was adapted from a 1998 essay written by a psychology graduate student exploring his heritage.

While my mother's parents spent their lives in New York, my paternal grandparents were born and raised in neighboring villages of Austria. My grandfather's father owned a liquor
5 store and was very religious. My grandfather was the academic of the family. He completed high school, college, and graduate degrees. He worked as a teacher and principal, much more respected positions then than now. I connected
10 deeply with this grandfather, Herman. He and I are sensitive, loving, prone to worry, and innately talented teachers.

Though my grandparents and great-grandparents were born in Austria, I am not Austrian. This, I
15 believe, is the case for many Jews in the United States. Belonging to this religion is a cultural heritage as well as a faith. Though I rarely think of myself as Jewish and pay small heed to the holidays, Judaism is a large part of my identity.

1 The main purpose of the passage is to

Ⓐ persuade.

Ⓑ inform.

Ⓒ apologize.

Ⓓ eulogize.

2 The narrator does not consider himself Austrian (line 14) because

Ⓐ his great-grandparents were not born there.

Ⓑ he does not think of himself as Jewish.

Ⓒ his grandfather left at a young age.

Ⓓ his religion defines his heritage.

3 In line 2, the word "paternal" most nearly means

Ⓐ great.

Ⓑ on my father's side.

Ⓒ on my mother's side.

Ⓓ adopted.

4 The author gives all of the following as support for his grandfather being an "academic" (line 6) EXCEPT

Ⓐ he was a talented teacher.

Ⓑ he completed graduate degrees.

Ⓒ he was prone to worry.

Ⓓ he worked as a principal.

5 What does the narrator imply in lines 18 and 19 by "pay small heed to the holidays"?

Ⓐ The narrator contributes very little money to religious organizations.

Ⓑ The narrator rarely observes Jewish holidays.

Ⓒ Judaism is a large part of the narrator's identity.

Ⓓ The narrator is not Jewish.

This passage is from a 2007 scientific paper that explores the water resources of the town of Meadville.

The city of Meadville is particularly well blessed in terms of water resources. The town's two municipal aquifers, the Cussewago sandstone bedrock aquifer and the glacial outwash aquifer,
5 are capable of producing a more than sufficient yield for industry and residents. The outwash aquifers exist mainly in the valleys and produce far better yields, since the thick drifts of sand and gravel are far more permeable.

10 The two most significant bedrock aquifers are found in Sharpsville Sandstone and in Cusswego Sandstone. The Meadville aquifers are recharged through precipitation. The recharge zone for these aquifers is large, consisting
15 of all ground areas within the groundwater divide of the French Creek valley watershed. Stream flow and groundwater levels are highest in early spring as snowmelt is discharged, and lowest in late summer, when precipitation
20 is low and evaporation high. Evaporation is particularly important since Woodcock Creek is influenced by the reservoir, and the water level of the reservoir changes from evaporation in warmer weather. French Creek and its tributar-
25 ies run through rural, subtropical terrain and, thusly, transpiration affects the hydrologic cycle significantly.

French Creek and the Meadville aquifer are recharged through precipitation, as has been said
30 before. But this isn't a simple process. Precipitation that falls anywhere within the French Creek valley, as long as it's on the correct side of the water divide, will end up in French Creek or in an aquifer eventually (and *eventually* in the At-
35 lantic Ocean). But how it gets there varies considerably. Some water will precipitate and enter the system promptly. Some will precipitate in the form of snow, and be released at a later time, usually in larger volume. Water traveling
40 from higher, more distant locations takes longer to reach French Creek than does water closer to the discharge area.

The table organizes certain facts about two of the Meadville aquifers.

	Components	Recharge
Sandstone bedrock	Sandstone, rock	Precipitation, snowmelt
Glacial outwash	Sand, gravel	Precipitation, snowmelt

6 From the italicized introductory material, the reader can assume that the primary tone of the passage as a whole will be

Ⓐ affectionate nostalgia.

Ⓑ awe and fear.

Ⓒ uncertainty and impatience.

Ⓓ analytical detachment.

7 The author's tone in the first sentence is best described as

Ⓐ joyous.

Ⓑ contemptuous.

Ⓒ diagnostic.

Ⓓ mischievous.

8 A major difference between paragraph 2 and paragraph 3 is

Ⓐ paragraph 3 explores a statement of paragraph 2 in greater detail.

Ⓑ paragraph 2 describes events that happened before those of paragraph 3.

Ⓒ paragraph 3 describes three types of aquifers.

Ⓓ paragraph 3 is more emotive.

9 The passage is primarily concerned with

Ⓐ the water supply shortage in Meadville.

Ⓑ Meadville's European exchange program.

Ⓒ Meadville's municipal budget.

Ⓓ how Meadville's water supply replenishes.

10 Which choice provides the best evidence for the answer to the previous question?

(A) line 1 ("The . . . resources")

(B) lines 24–27 ("French . . . significantly")

(C) lines 28–30 ("French . . . before")

(D) lines 35 and 36 ("But . . . considerably")

11 Based on the table and the passage, why does the outwash aquifer produce better yields?

(A) Sand and gravel allow more water to pass through.

(B) Bedrock is less permeable.

(C) Sandstone and bedrock allow the free flow of water.

(D) The passage and the table do not indicate why the outwash aquifer produces better yields.

12 The parentheses around "and *eventually* in the Atlantic Ocean" (lines 34 and 35) serve to

(A) emphasize the vast size of the Atlantic Ocean.

(B) criticize Meadville's water politics.

(C) indicate that the information is interesting but inessential.

(D) demonstrate the geological significance of Meadville.

13 Which of the following is an example of "Some water will precipitate and enter the system promptly" described in lines 36 and 37?

(A) Water treated in an adjacent plant

(B) Rain that falls directly on the area

(C) Snow that falls in the aquifer

(D) Water that evaporated at high altitudes

14 The passage is primarily

(A) a reflection on an educational journey.

(B) a dispassionate plea for government funding to save an endangered aquifer.

(C) a report on a water system.

(D) a criticism of water resource management in Meadville.

Each passage below is accompanied by a number of questions. For some questions, you will consider how the passage might be revised to improve the expression of ideas. For other questions, you will consider how the passage might be edited to correct errors in sentence structure, usage, or punctuation. A passage or a question may be accompanied by one or more graphics (such as a table or graph) that you will consider as you make revising and editing decisions.

Some questions will direct you to an underlined portion of a passage. Other questions will direct you to a location in a passage or ask you to think about the passage as a whole.

After reading each passage, choose the answer to each question that most effectively improves the quality of writing in the passage or that makes the passage conform to the conventions of standard written English. Many questions include a "NO CHANGE" option. Choose that option if you think the best choice is to leave the relevant portion of the passage as it is.

One early August day last year, I have been waking
                                         15
up to the rapid flapping of wings and the agitated
high-pitched cry of my cat Hissy. She, with no results,
were trying to catch a frightened bat. I yelped,
    16
scrambled out of my bed, grabbed little Hissy, and
slammed my bedroom door shut.

I barged into Jenna and Sapphire's room, and
begged her to get it out of my room. They got up
        17
and put towels at the bottom of my door so the
sly bat could not escape into the house. Therefore,
                                            18
Jenna went outside and climbed up to my roof and
opened my window a crack, unaware of where
the bat was lurking. Would the bat attack her,
would it hide, or fly out? That bat was fierce, but
                 19

15 Ⓐ NO CHANGE
    Ⓑ waking
    Ⓒ woke
    Ⓓ had been waked

16 Ⓐ NO CHANGE
    Ⓑ was
    Ⓒ trying
    Ⓓ was trying

17 Ⓐ NO CHANGE
    Ⓑ them
    Ⓒ it
    Ⓓ its

18 Ⓐ NO CHANGE
    Ⓑ Then,
    Ⓒ Still
    Ⓓ However

19 Ⓐ NO CHANGE
    Ⓑ or would it fly out
    Ⓒ or flying out
    Ⓓ or it be flying out

Jenna was certainly as fierce. My mother and I, sat

20   21

anxiously watching Jenna. We waited for a long
time, and then Jenna finally decided to climb
into the room to check the situation. Apparently
the bat had flown out without any of us even
noticing. The relief was overwhelming. We had
no idea, however, about the shots to come.

22

The following day, we called the doctor's office and
asked if there was anything we had to do since I
had woken up about a bat in my room. Then, the

23

news came. I needed rabies shots so that I wouldn't
be foaming at the mouth or anything like that.
"It's awful news," my mom agreed.

24

I went to the Emergency Room to get my first round
of shots. I went in and lay down in a bed and waited.
The nurses' came in and said that in that one day, I

25

would have to be getting four shots: two shots in my

26

butt, two shots in my arms!

20 (A) NO CHANGE
    (B) Jenna being
    (C) Jenna would have been
    (D) Jenna's skills are

21 (A) NO CHANGE
    (B) and, I sat
    (C) and I sat,
    (D) and me, sat,

22 (A) NO CHANGE
    (B) idea; however, about
    (C) idea, however about
    (D) idea however about

23 (A) NO CHANGE
    (B) woken up with
    (C) woken up in
    (D) woken up from

24 (A) NO CHANGE
    (B) Its awful
    (C) That being awful
    (D) It being awful

25 (A) NO CHANGE
    (B) nurse's came
    (C) nurses' coming
    (D) nurses came

26 (A) NO CHANGE
    (B) get to be having
    (C) be having to be getting
    (D) have to get

156

The pain was agonizing. Having trouble finding my vein, the nurse had to inject me three times.
                                              27
I ended up passing out right after the first shot.

After waking up, I got more bad news. I would have to go get more rabies vaccines, nine total!

That month was dreadful. I would sit for hours in the Emergency Room, waiting greatly for my name
                                                                                    28
to be called. Once when I was there, the Emergency

Room was so crowded that the nurse giving me the shot simply put me on a rolling computer chair in the middle of the Emergency Room. The nurse started to give me the shot, but then I passed out and started rolling down the hallway in the
                                              29
computer chair! They had people running after me,
                                              29
trying to catch me.
        29

30 Every time I would go, they would say, "Hey, it's rabies girl." Even the kids in my high school picked up on it. It's not my favorite nickname, but I guess it has character.

31 When I had finished my rabies series,

27 (A) NO CHANGE
   (B) vein, I was injected
   (C) injections were given to me
   (D) vein, the nurse had to be injecting me

28 (A) NO CHANGE
   (B) deeply
   (C) anxiously
   (D) intensely

29 If the writer were to delete the underlined portion, the paragraph would lose
   (A) a tie-in to the introduction
   (B) a transition from one sentence to the next
   (C) a comical anecdote
   (D) nothing at all, since this sentence is out of place

30 Which of the following true statements would best introduce the tone and focus of this paragraph?
   (A) After that crazy day, I had a new nickname.
   (B) I was invincible after surviving the shots.
   (C) Boy, those shots hurt!
   (D) I never passed out from the shots again.

31 Suppose the author had intended for the final paragraph to serve as a conclusion for the essay. Would the paragraph fulfill this goal?
   (A) Yes, because the paragraph provides many details about the rabies shots.
   (B) Yes, because the paragraph wraps up the writer's rabies shots experience and describes her lesson from the experience.
   (C) No, because the paragraph does not wrap up the essay as a whole.
   (D) No, because the paragraph lacks sufficient details to back up its claim.

I felt invincibly . A pro I was now at getting shots.
　　　32　　　　　33
I could go up to any animal I wanted. And I
wouldn't get rabies. 34 And, even though I haven't
hugged any raccoons in the past fourteen months,
today I was felt stronger and braver than ever.
　　　　　35

32　Ⓐ NO CHANGE
　　　Ⓑ had a feeling of invincible
　　　Ⓒ felt invincible
　　　Ⓓ feel invincibly

33　Ⓐ NO CHANGE
　　　Ⓑ I was a pro now
　　　Ⓒ A pro feeling I now had
　　　Ⓓ A pro I am now

34　What is the best way to combine the two sen-
　　　tences reproduced below?

　　　And I could go up to any animal I wanted. And
　　　I wouldn't get rabies.

　　　Ⓐ And I could go up to any animal I wanted
　　　　　without getting rabies.
　　　Ⓑ Therefore I could go up to any animal I
　　　　　wanted; without getting rabies.
　　　Ⓒ And I could go up to any animal I wanted, I
　　　　　wouldn't get rabies.
　　　Ⓓ And I could go up to any animal I wanted in
　　　　　the full knowledge of not getting rabies.

35　Ⓐ NO CHANGE
　　　Ⓑ am felt
　　　Ⓒ feel
　　　Ⓓ been feeling

Skills 36 to 50: Essay

See Essay prompt on next page.

Bonus:

The morning of the test you should

Ⓐ eat as huge a breakfast as you can stuff into
　　your face.
Ⓑ eat a normal (healthy) breakfast.
Ⓒ drink 4 Jolt colas for energy.
Ⓓ leave your house without your ID, calcula-
　　tor, pencils, and admission slip.

Essay

Time: 50 minutes

As you read the passage below, consider how the author uses:

> - Evidence, such as facts or examples, to support claims.
> - Reasoning to develop ideas and to connect claims and evidence.
> - Stylistic or persuasive elements, such as word choice or appeals to emotion, to add power to the ideas expressed.

Adapted from Mahatma Gandhi's "Quit India" speech, delivered August 8, 1942.

Before you discuss the resolution, let me place before you one or two things, I want you to understand two things very clearly and to consider them from the same point of view from which I am placing them before you. I ask you to consider it from my point of view, because if you approve of it, you will be enjoined to carry out all I say. It will be a great responsibility. There are people who ask me whether I am the same man that I was in 1920, or whether there has been any change in me. You are right in asking that question.

Let me, however, hasten to assure that I am the same Gandhi as I was in 1920. I have not changed in any fundamental respect. I attach the same importance to non-violence that I did then. If at all, my emphasis on it has grown stronger. There is no real contradiction between the present resolution and my previous writings and utterances.

Ours is not a drive for power, but purely a non-violent fight for India's independence. In a violent struggle, a successful general has been often known to effect a military coup and to set up a dictatorship. But under the Congress scheme of things, essentially non-violent as it is, there can be no room for dictatorship. A non-violent soldier of freedom will covet nothing for himself, he fights only for the freedom of his country. The Congress is unconcerned as to who will rule, when freedom is attained. The power, when it comes, will belong to the people of India, and it will be for them to decide to whom it placed in the entrusted. May be that the reins will be placed in the hands of the Parsis, for instance—as I would love to see happen—or they may be handed to some others whose names are not heard in the Congress today. It will not be for you then to object saying, "This community is microscopic. That party did not play its due part in the freedom's struggle; why should it have all the power?" Ever since its inception the Congress has kept itself meticulously free of the communal taint. It has thought always in terms of the whole nation and has acted accordingly. . . . I know how imperfect our Ahimsa is and how far away we are still from the ideal, but in Ahimsa there is no final failure or defeat. I have faith, therefore, that if, in spite of our shortcomings, the big thing does happen, it will be because God wanted to help us by crowning with success our silent, unremitting Sadhana for the last twenty-two years. I believe that in the history of the world, there has not been a more genuinely democratic struggle for freedom than ours. I read Carlyle's French Revolution while I was in prison, and Pandit Jawaharlal has told me something about the Russian revolution. But it is my conviction that inasmuch as these struggles were fought with the weapon of violence they failed to realize the democratic ideal. In the democracy which I have envisaged, a democracy established by non-violence, there will be equal freedom for all. Everybody will be his own master. It is to join a struggle for such democracy that I invite you today. Once you realize this you will forget the differences between the Hindus and Muslims, and think of yourselves as Indians only, engaged in the common struggle for independence.

Then, there is the question of your attitude towards the British. I have noticed that there is hatred towards the British among the people. The people say they are disgusted with their behaviour. The people make no distinction between British imperialism and the British people. To them, the two are one. This hatred would even make them welcome the Japanese. It is most dangerous. It means that they will exchange one slavery for another. We must get rid of this feeling. Our quarrel is not with the British people, we fight their imperialism. The proposal for the withdrawal of British power did not come out of anger. It came to enable India to play its due part at the present critical juncture. It is not a happy position for a big country like India to be merely helping with money and material obtained willy-nilly from her while the United Nations are conducting the war. We cannot evoke the true spirit of sacrifice and valour, so long as we are not free. I know the British Government will not be able to withhold freedom from us, when we have made enough self-sacrifice. We must, therefore, purge ourselves of hatred. Speaking for myself, I can say that I have never felt any hatred. As a matter of fact, I feel myself to be a greater friend of the British now than ever before. One reason is that they are today in distress. My very friendship, therefore, demands that I should try to save them from their mistakes. As I view the situation, they are on the brink of an abyss. It, therefore, becomes my duty to warn them of their danger even though it may, for the time being, anger them to the point of cutting off the friendly hand that is stretched out to help them. People may laugh, nevertheless that is my claim. At a time when I may have to launch the biggest struggle of my life, I may not harbor hatred against anybody.

Write an essay in which you explain how the author builds an argument to persuade his audience for determined but passive resistance to gain India's independence. In your essay, analyze how the author uses one or more of the features listed in the box above (or features of your own choice) to strengthen the logic and persuasiveness of his argument. Be sure that your analysis focuses on the most relevant features of the passage.

Solutions

Reading Comprehension

Skill 1 (page 19)

The Intro Paragraph

1. Both passages are about environmentalism, and both are fairly recent. The second passage was written more recently and is about the environmentalism of the 1970s. We pretty much know the main idea of both passages. Now we would just need to pay attention to the tone of each.

2. This is from a fairly recent novel, and women are discussing relationships. This might not seem like much, but it's a big leg up toward knowing the main idea of the passage. With this info alone, I bet we could eliminate three choices on a main idea question.

3. A 1990s article that describes new medical technologies; written by a doctor. The passage might use science terms, but don't be intimidated. The SAT always defines any science terms in the passage.

4. Both passages are about *Roe v. Wade*, an important and controversial case that legalized abortion. Since both are about the same topic, they probably take slightly different angles toward it.

5. It was written in 1820, so it's older and, being from of a different time period, possibly more "proper." Mr. Peabody wants to date Mrs. Primberly's daughter, Josephine. This is quite a bit of info, probably enough to answer any main idea question.

6. Discusses changes brought about by CDs and MP3 players. Probably a fairly unbiased account, since it's written by an historian.

Skill 2 (page 21)

The SAT Reading Meditation

1. Main idea: The author is describing his heritage.

   Point/tone: Author is giving insight into his heritage.

2. Notice that this passage does not begin with italics. Some short passages do not begin with italics. This is a great passage to practice with because many students are initially intimidated by its fancy language. But the beginning and end of the passage directly state the main idea. If you get intimidated when you are looking for the main idea, just keep reading and pay close attention to the beginning and end of the passage.

   Main idea: Law is not just a set of rules, but also the pursuit of justice and fairness.

   Point/tone: The author is **describing** information in a **neutral** way.

Skill 3 (page 23)

"Plethora" Most Nearly Means

1. **B** The author is using "flair" here to mean "appeal" or "style," but goes on to write about fire and light, so choices A and C seem like good choices. However, choice B is correct; "panache" means "spirited style" or "flair." Another great SAT synonym for flair is "élan."

   If you are unsure, treat this like a sentence completion question. Choices A and C do not work because they do not fit the meaning of the sentence.

2. **C** Line 9 mentions that she fed their (referring to the public) adoration with her poems, so the "public" refers to her readers.

3. **D** The three words before "nature" are "charismatic," "headstrong," and "passionate," and these describe Millay's personality. Use the process of elimination. The best fit is "spirit."

4. **A** The previous lines stated that the public adored her. She fed this adoration by writing her poems. "Adoration" means "love," and the closest answer here is "respect."

5. **A** The next sentence tells us that her father left the family, they were very poor, and her mom worked hard, so "bleak" must mean "tough" or "harsh." "Austere" means "harsh." Other great SAT synonyms for austere are "stark," "spartan," and "ascetic." "Bland" is incorrect because we have no evidence from the passage that her childhood was dull.

6. **C** All of these choices have been mentioned in the passage, but in the context of the sentence, "the others" are her siblings, of whom she is the oldest.

7. **B** The paragraph describes an austere (harsh) childhood. Use the process of elimination; remember, sometimes you find the best answer not because it jumps right out at you, but by eliminating the others.

   Ⓐ ~~twisted~~—No; it wasn't warped, it was just tough.

   Ⓑ wan—If you don't know the word, leave it. "Wan" means "pale," so maybe.

   Ⓒ ~~evil~~—No; it was a tough childhood, but it wasn't evil.

   Ⓓ ~~virtuous~~—No, "virtuous" means "honorable," vibe it out with the word "virtue."

Eliminate the ones that you can, and then pick the best of what's left. Even if you are not right every time, you will be right more than before and will gain points!

Skill 4 (page 27)

Direct Info

1. **D** The "three stages of life" refer to "three ways of being in the world." This is shown in the first sentence, where the author states that the stages are not "youth, adulthood, and old age," but "three modes of relating to the world."

2. **B** When you answer a line number question, always read a little before and after that line. The answer to this question comes directly after the reference. The passage refers to "the first and third poems" as "internal" and the second poem as "external."

3. **B** Great question! The phrase "passing elegiacally over the lore of the land" seems tough. Many kids will throw up their hands and move on, but the phrase is clearly explained in the next line: "The dying poet is taking a nostalgic survey of his works." He is looking back and "taking stock." It's easy if you stay with it and don't get thrown by tough language.

4. **A** The sentence referred to might seem confusing or unclear, but just read what comes before and after and it's clear! The previous sentence states that "If this passing is to have any meaning," he must "find the memories in which he was most alive."

5. **C** This comes directly from the poem. In line 14, the author refers to the poem as a ceremony.

Skill 5 (page 29)

What Are You Trying to Suggest?

1. **D** The "changes" help a person to successfully engage or run from a physical threat (material danger), not to deal with intellectual challenges, so choice D is best. This is nearly a "direct info" question.

2. **D** The problems listed are intellectual. Therefore, we can infer that they are not solved by the stress response, which only helps a person to fight or to flee. Choice B is incorrect because, while the passage states that these problems can persist, it does not give that as a reason for the stress response not solving them.

3. **A** The last paragraph states that the goal of stress management is to experience the stress response **only** when it is relevant and helpful, implying that it is to be avoided when it cannot help.

4. **(D)** This "attitude" question is a specific type of "suggest" question that we will address more fully in Skill 7. We also predicted this question when we initially read the passage, reading for main idea and tone. The answer to an "attitude" question is usually moderate. Rarely, on the SAT, does the author hate or love something. Let's take a look at the choices:

(A) ~~qualified disapproval~~—No, the author shows no disapproval.

(B) ~~resentment~~—No; again, there's no resentment.

(C) ambivalence—Maybe, but the author does not seem wishy-washy.

(D) unbiased appreciation—Yes, the author seems to be presenting an unbiased account. Also, since we know from the italics that the passage is from a master's thesis, we can assume that it is scholarly and unbiased, not opinionated and biased.

Skill 6 (page 31)

ASS of U and ME

1. **(B)** In line 1, the author is making a generalization that assumes that "others" do not understand the complexity of polarity. To find the best answer, think of the answer you'd like to see and use the process of elimination. While choice B is not worded the way I would have put it, it is the best choice available, and even the only choice that works. That's why elimination works so well. Choice C is tempting, but the passage states that people misunderstand, not that they are not interested.

2. **(A)** The author states that "in one of the greatest minds . . . one might expect a preference for knowledge over creativity, or hard work over play." He is stating that people might assume that Einstein was all about hard work instead of intuition, creativity, and play. Using the process of elimination, you can get this question, even if you didn't know the fancy vocab word "assiduous."

3. **(B)** Use the process of elimination. The paragraph is based on the assumption that science and religion are considered opposites. The whole point of the paragraph is to counter this assumption and demonstrate that they go hand in hand. So answer choice A might be the main idea of the paragraph, but choice B is the assumption.

4. **(D)** Reread the lines before and after any "line number" question. The answer is found after line 1, in line 4, "opposites." You can also treat it like a sentence completion; think of a word that you'd like to see, and then use the process of elimination with the choices. Remember that the answer to this type of question will rarely be the easiest and most obvious of the answer choices that you might choose without having read the passage.

Vocabulary Special Section I

Compliment or Insult?

a. peevish—irritable
b. petulant—irritable
c. sophisticated—stylish
d. soporific—sleep-inducing
e. saccharine—sugary
f. bombastic—showy, pretentious, conceited
g. magnificent—wonderful
h. abased—belittled
i. astute—shrewd, perceptive
j. flippant—offhand, jokey
k. enthralling—interesting, gripping
l. vapid—insipid, bland
m. diminutive—very small
n. salutary—helpful
o. magnanimous—generous
p. insipid—dull
q. sagacious—wise
r. baneful—destructive
s. dazzling—stunning
t. resolute—determined
u. pernicious—harmful
v. disingenuous—insincere, devious, dishonest
w. truculent—aggressive, obstreperous, hostile
x. diverting—fun
y. corrupt—crooked
z. charismatic—charming, appealing

Vocabulary Special Section II

Superbad Vocabulary

1. *Lord of the Rings: The Fellowship of the Ring* (New Line Cinema, 2001). "Malice" means "hatred."

2. *Star Wars: Episode VI—Return of the Jedi* (20th Century Fox, Lucasfilm Ltd., 1983). "Imminent" means "about to happen, looming."

3. *Pirates of the Caribbean: The Curse of the Black Pearl* (Walt Disney, 2003). "Negotiate" means "discuss" or "parley." "Cessation" means "end" or "termination." "Hostilities" means "fighting" or "aggression." "Naught" means "not anything." "Humble" means "modest." "Disinclined" means "reluctant." "Acquiesce" means "give in" or "assent, comply, concede, or yield."

4. *Wedding Crashers* (New Line Cinema, 2005). "Erroneous" means "incorrect."

5. *Monty Python and the Holy Grail* (20th Century Fox, 1975). "Temperate" means "mild" or "moderate." The SAT loves to say that something tempered or temporizes something, meaning makes more mild.

6. *Pirates of the Caribbean: Curse of the Black Pearl* (Walt Disney, 2003). "Superfluous" means "not required." "Nigh" means "near."

7. *Star Wars: Episode IV—A New Hope* (20th Century Fox, Lucasfilm Ltd., 1977). "Protocol" means "etiquette" or "rules governing polite behavior."

8. *Ferris Bueller's Day Off* (Paramount Pictures, 1986). "Socialism" is a political theory in which the people collectively own all property. "Fascist" means "an authoritarian system of government." "Anarchist" means "revolutionary." "Condone" means "allow" or "pardon." "-Ism" means "a practice or philosophy."

9. *Harry Potter and the Order of the Phoenix* (Warner Bros., 2007). "Implore" means "beg." Great synonyms: "beseech" and "entreat." "Incontrovertible" means "unquestionable." Great SAT synonyms: "irrefutable," "indubitable," "unassailable," "indisputable."

10. *Iron Man* (Paramount Pictures, 2008). "Incinerate" means "burn." "Nostalgic" means "wistful" or "remembering fondly."

Vocabulary Special Section III

Deodorant and Spanish Class

1. "Diverting" includes the Spanish word "divertir," which means "to entertain." That's perfect because in English, "diverting" means "fun."

2. "Facile" sounds a lot like the Spanish for "easy." That's great, 'cause in English it means "very easy."

3. "Luminance" sounds a lot like the French word "lumière" for light. Good, because in English it's a fancy word meaning "the condition of emitting or reflecting light."

4. "Clairvoyant" sounds like the French words "clair," meaning "clear," and "voyant," meaning "seeing." Does "clairvoyant" mean "clear seeing"? Yep, pretty much, or at least enough to get a sentence completion question right. It means "someone who sees things beyond normal vision."

5. In French, "comportment" means "behavior," which is exactly what it means in English!

6. In French, "fille" means "daughter," which is a pretty good lead, since in English, "filial" means "pertaining to a son or daughter."

7. "Arid" was actually another word that was on my SAT. I didn't know it, but I remembered a TV commercial jingle for the antiperspirant deodorant Arrid Extra Dry. I thought, "If Arrid is the name of a deodorant, there's no way it means 'smelly' or 'foul' or 'wet' or anything bad. It must mean 'smells good' or 'dry' or 'attractive,'" and that was enough to vibe the word and get the question correct. "Arid" means "very dry."

8. The Impervious Charm is the one that makes things repel substances like water, and "impervious" means "impermeable" or "resistant."

9. "Stupefy" is the Stunning Spell that stuns an opponent, and "stupefy" means "bewilder" or "stun."

10. In *Harry Potter*, "flagrate" causes a wand to leave fiery marks, and the word "conflagration" means "a fire."

11. "Sagacious" means "wise," like a sage.

12. If your intelligence is 16 or better, you might know that Sylvan is the language of the Elves. And "sylvan" is a great SAT word that means "pertaining to the forest."

13. I was psyched when this word showed up on the SAT; you know they game! When you need to get out fast, Expeditious Retreat is a cheap potion and an easy first-level wizard spell. "Expeditious" means "speedy."

Vocabulary Special Section IV

Splitting Words

1. sympathy—understanding
   empathy—compassion
   apathy—lack of concern
   pathos—grief
   pathetic—pitiable
   antipathy—bad feelings, hatred
   "path" means "feeling"
   "a" means "not" or "without"
   "anti" means "against"

2. philanthropy—love for humankind or generosity
   philosophy—love of knowledge or a system of thought
   technophile—a person who likes technology
   technophobe—a person who fears technology
   technology—the study of devices
   phobia—a fear
   "phil" means "love"
   "anthro" means "humans"
   "soph" means "knowledge"

"tech" means "devices or tools"
"phobe" means "fear"
"ology" means "study of"

3. terrestrial—relating to the earth
   terrain—ground
   extraterrestrial—from beyond the earth
   extraordinary—beyond the ordinary
   "terr" means "earth"
   "extra" means "beyond"

4. homogeneous—having the same nature
   heterogeneous—having a different nature
   homologous—sharing the same structure or origin
   heterologous—differing in structure or origin
   homosexual—attracted to one's own gender
   heterosexual—attracted to the opposite gender
   "homo" means "same"
   "hetero" means "different"
   "gen" means "kind" or "birth"

5. circumscribe—to draw around
   circumnavigate—to sail or fly around
   circumvent—to get around something
   recirculate—to circulate again
   postscript—something written at the end of something
   transcribe—to translate
   circumambulate—to walk around something
   amble—walk
   manuscript—something written (technically by hand)
   manufacture—to make something (technically by hand)
   transatlantic—across the Atlantic Ocean
   "circum" means "around"
   "post" means "after"
   "scribe" means "write"
   "man" means "hand"
   "re" means "again"
   "trans" means "across"
   "amb" means "walk"
   "dis" means "not," like distrust = not trust
   "co" means "together," like cooperate = operate together
   "sub" means "under," like submarine = underwater

Skill 7 (page 45)

Some Attitude

1. **A** The intro paragraph helps a lot; the speaker is mourning the loss of Donny. If you are unsure, use the process of elimination and choose the best choice. Even if you don't know the word "eulogy," you can get it through elimination.

2. **A** The first line reads, "Donny was a good bowler, and a good man." The speaker relates the two and considers bowling very important. Then he says, "He was one of us." He respects bowling. Remember to answer based on the passage, not on your opinion of bowling!

3. **D** The speaker is upset (not "ambivalent," which means "unsure") that these men died before "their time," but he is not bitter. He is resigned, which means "accepting." If you are not sure, use the process of elimination. And remember to answer based on this passage, not on your opinion, and not based on Walter's body language as he delivers this in *The Big Lebowski*, if you've seen it! (Great movie that I highly recommend!)

4. **C** "Solemn" means "somber" or "serious." The speaker is serious and mournful. This was given away in the intro paragraph, since we knew from the start that he was scattering ashes. Don't be confused by "what we think your dying wishes might well have been." He is a doof, but he's primarily not confused. He's solemn.

5. **B** "Bright" could means any of the answer choices, but in the passage, it describes Donny and the young men that the speaker mourns who died at the battles mentioned. Choice B is the best; they were intelligent: "flowering young men." You can treat this like a sentence completion; think of a word that you'd like to see, and then use the process of elimination with the choices. Remember that the answer to this type of question will rarely be the easiest and most obvious of the answer choices, the

one that you might choose without having read the passage.

6. **D** Treat this like a sentence completion. Think of a word that you'd like to see, and then use the process of elimination with the choices. Remember that the answer to this type of question will rarely be the easiest and most obvious of the answer choices, the one that you might choose without having read the passage. "Comfort" is the only choice that works; they are scattering his ashes there for him to "rest in peace."

7. **D** The speaker is eulogizing his friend Donny as he scatters his ashes. In doing so, he remembers others that he has lost and digresses to them for a moment. The line suggests that he misses them as he misses Donny. Remember that the key to a "suggest" question is not to overthink it. You could convince yourself of any of the answers, but only choice D has evidence and makes sense in the passage.

Skill 8 (page 47)

Two Passages

1. **B** Usually there are a few questions that ask about only the first passage. That's why you first read only the first passage and answer those questions before you even read the second passage. In this case, that eliminates choices C and D, which are not even mentioned in Passage 1. The other choices are mentioned in the passage, but only pharmaceuticals is cited as an example of a biochemical medicine. This is a "direct info" type of question. Just find the proof. If you do, you can't go wrong!

2. **B** This is a very literal question. Just use the process of elimination and check each choice to see if the author used it or not. Passage 2 uses generalizations, defines a term, and cites an authority, but it does not refute a hypothesis, so Choice B is correct.

3. **C** This is a classic "two-passage" question. After you read the first passage, jot down or circle a word or two that identify both the main

idea and the tone; and after you read the second passage, do the same. This helps you keep their differences and similarities clear. The author of Passage 1 mentions three systems and details the biochemical system. The author of Passage 2 describes the Indian system of Ayurveda as a natural and holistic medical system that considers a "whole substance." The biochemical model is described as isolating an active ingredient, so Ayurveda is not biochemical and the author of Passage 1 would consider it either bioenergetic or biospiritual.

4. **B** Use the process of elimination. The only choice that is encouraged in both passages is consideration of the whole effect of medicines on the body. Passage 1 describes biochemical medicine and states that a drawback of isolated active ingredients can be unanticipated side effects. Passage 2 discusses Ayurveda, which considers the whole effect of a medicine on a person. Don't overthink and choose choice C. Perhaps Passage 1 alludes very lightly to medical reform, but Passage 2 never mentions it at all.

5. **A** As you read the second passage, you can pretty much predict all of these choices. You are watching for what is the same and what is different. We know the SAT will ask these questions. Use the process of elimination. I like this type of question. It is like a two-blank sentence completion; we can eliminate a choice if either part of it is wrong. Here we can eliminate the choice if it is incorrect about either passage. Choice A is correct, since the main idea of the first passage is the three-system model and the second passage is about only one system.

Skill 9 (page 49)

Main Idea

1. **B** Most of the choices are mentioned in the passage, but the main idea, the primary purpose of the passage, is to demonstrate Olmsted's vision. Let's find evidence: it is demonstrated by the words "foresaw," "anticipated," and "see into the future."

2. **C** This is an interesting case; all are possible at first glance. But only choice C is correct. Here's the evidence:

   (A) depict an era—Nope; it does not depict an era, just a particular situation.

   (B) justify an expenditure—Nope; the author cites Gustave's justification, but that is not the author's point.

   (C) give an historical account—Yes, it is the account of Parisians' response to the building of the Eiffel Tower.

   (D) defend a decision—No, the author cites Gustave defending his decision, but that is not the author's point.

3. **C** Find the evidence. It seems as if the author is recollecting, but "If we had this tree . . ." proves that it is actually a fantasy.

Skill 10 (page 51)

Best Evidence

1. **D** If you're unsure of the answer to this question, use the next one, the "best evidence" question, to find the answer.

2. **C** Lines 61–64 (Regular sugar consumption . . . natural reward high) answer the previous question.

3. **B** If you're unsure of the answer to this question, use the next one, the "best evidence" question, to find the answer.

4. **B** Lines 47–49 (But a sweet taste . . . clean energy!) answer the previous question.

Skill 11 (page 55)

Table

1. **D** Lines 53–55 in the passage state that "Until recently, with the advent of the brownie that beat the system and messed everything up," which is supported by the data in that table, that the sugar content in the brownie far exceeds the sugar content in an apple or grapes.

2. **C** This is a great review of Skill 10. Choice C lists the grams of sugar for the apple, grapes, and brownie.

3. **A** The ratios for the three foods are apple 8.8/44 (approximately 1/5), grapes 13.2/57 (approximately 1/4), and brownie 42/396 (approximately 1/9). The brownie has, by far, the lowest ratio.

4. **C** The passage states that brownies are a recent addition to the human diet.

Skill 12 (page 57)

Gretchen Is "Such" a Good Friend

1. **A** The misspelled words simulate the narrator's accent. This is a cool "don't overthink it" question. Use the process of elimination. There is no evidence for choice B, "indicate his disapproval of the accepted spellings," or choices C and D.

2. **B** Use the process of elimination. We have evidence only for choice B. When the author writes, there's "a name no man would self-apply," he is reiterating his opinion of the unusualness of the name. Remember that quotes around a word on the SAT that are not used to simply cite a source usually indicate that the word is meant in an unusual way.

3. **A** Use the process of elimination. No other answer makes any sense with the passage. The repetition of the lines is used to demonstrate that the narrator is losing focus.

4. **C** Treat this type of question very literally.

   (A) a hypothesis and supporting details—Nope; there's no hypothesis and no support for it.

   (B) a common argument following by counterexamples to disprove it—No, nothing is being disproved.

   (C) description interspersed with tangential remarks—Yes, there's lots of description and lots of tangential (unrelated) remarks.

   (D) several sides to a single issue—No, there's no presentation of several sides.

5. **D** Treat this like a sentence completion question. Reread the lines around it and think of a word that will fill the blank. Then use the process of elimination. In this case, "handle" refers to "name" in the previous line, so "title" is the best answer. Remember that the answer is not usually the word that you would pick without having read the passage, such as "handle" meaning "grip."

6. **C** This is a "direct info" question. The phrase explains the one before it, "See, they call Los Angeles the 'City of Angels.'" So he is saying that even though it's called "City of Angels," he didn't exactly meet "angels."

Skill 13 (page 61)

Parallel

1. **A** The lines say that the media makes people think that they have to be fit and wealthy and to own things. Use the process of elimination. Choice A fits this situation best.

2. **C** The passage describes a situation that the writer finds unacceptable. He or she riles up readers and ends with an alternative. Probably, the writer will next give more info about the alternative. You can also use the process of elimination; certain other answer choices use words from the passage, but they do not fit the nature of the passage.

3. **B** Use the process of elimination and remember that you are looking for the alternative that **least** undermines the assertion that 2.5 hours of TV per day is not making people happy and that it confuses people by skewing their expectations of life. What would detract from this assertion least? Basically, an example that supports that idea, rather than refutes it. Anything opposite would disprove or detract from it and would not be the answer. So the best answer is choice B. Choice B supports the idea that people believe the messages they see on TV. All the other answers do not support the assertion and therefore detract more from it.

4. **D** The tone of a passage is expressed in the words and punctuation. This passage is pointing out problems with media and television in society. The author is angry, but controls the anger in expressing his or her point. You can also use the process of elimination. None of the other choices work. The author is not laughing, confused, or relieved.

Skill 14 (page 66)

How to Be a Reading Ninja

1. Main idea question (Skill 9). D. As the first and last lines of the paragraphs ("pursuing a dream," "pursue what they love") clearly demonstrate, choice D ("follow their hearts") is the best answer—the other choices do show up in the passage, but only choice D is the **main point** of the passage. We can use several Skills here. Since this is a "main idea" question; it's not a bad idea to skip it and come back after you've done the line number questions; by then you'll know the passage even better. When you answer it, you can also reread the intro paragraph and the first and last lines of each paragraph for clues to the main idea. Then come up with a main idea you'd like to see and use the process of elimination. Also avoid the careless error of choosing an answer based on only a few words; make sure the whole answer makes sense.

2. "Such" a good friend question (Skill 12). A. This type of question asks why the author chose quote marks, parentheses, or a certain word or sentence to accomplish something. Use the process of elimination

   (A) to indicate a side comment to the reader—Sure, that makes sense.

   (B) ~~to indicate that it is unimportant~~—Nope; if it was unimportant, it would be left out.

   (C) ~~to indicate a humorous tone~~—No, it's not funny!

   (D) ~~to indicate a shift in meaning~~—No, there's no change in meaning.

3. "Direct info" question (Skill 4). D. Go back and read a few sentences before and after. The answer comes several times, most clearly a few lines before. Trident dislikes Eric solely because he is human—a different species. You can also use the process of elimination. No other answer makes sense.

4. "Parallel" question (Skill 13). C. The question asks which of the answers best illustrates the assertion "Disney is encouraging children to question preconceived ideas that we may have against a certain group." Use the process of elimination. Only choice C describes a plot line that clearly involves someone questioning preconceived ideas, she is **overcoming** her fear of snakes. You could try to overthink this one and argue that one of the other answers might set the stage for overcoming previously held beliefs, but only choice C directly states it. This type of question often throws kids when there are choices that they do not recognize from the passage. Remember, a "parallel" question usually provides choices that are not from the passage, and you need to decide which one would illustrate the point from the passage.

5. "Suggests" question (Skill 7). B. Reread a few sentences before and after the line. Look for evidence. She screams, "So much for true love" victoriously. "Victoriously" indicates that she considers beating "true love" a victory, so we have evidence for choice B, she is mocking "true love." Don't overthink this and go for choice A, C, or D. We have no evidence for these. Choice B is closest to the evidence in the passage—it is the most literal interpretation. Remember that a "suggests" question will often have an answer worded slightly differently from the wording in the passage, but the meaning should be the same. In fact, beware of choices with wording that comes directly from the passage—they are not always wrong, but double-check them.

6. "Most nearly means" question (Skill 3). C. Choice C is best, since Eric did not "love," "succeed," or "squash" Ursula; he "bested"

or "defeated" her. Treat this like a sentence completion question. Think of a word that you'd like to see replace "vanquishing" in the sentence. Then use the process of elimination on the choices. Eliminate only if you are sure a choice does not fit. Then choose the best answer. If you can't think of a word that you'd like to see, you can try each choice for "vanquishing" and see which one works.

7. "Attitude" question (Skill 7). D. Attitude is expressed in words and punctuation. The author repeatedly expresses respect for the valuable lessons that Disney gives children in *The Little Mermaid*. You can also use the process of elimination.

   Ⓐ frustration—Nope, no frustration.

   Ⓑ stoicism—Nope, the author is not "stoical" or "unemotional."

   Ⓒ wonder—Maybe.

   Ⓓ respect—Yes, the author respects Disney's lessons.

   Don't be fooled by choice C. "Wonder" is associated with Disney's movies, but that is definitely not the author's point or attitude. Remember to answer questions based on the passage, not on your own opinions.

Writing Multiple-Choice

Skill 15 (page 71)

Subject/Verb Agreement

1. Ⓒ Trust your ear. "Being it" sounds terrible. Try the choices. "Is it" is the only choice that sounds good. Choice B sounds very awkward, especially when you read the whole sentence. Choice D sounds weird because it's missing a verb.

2. Ⓐ No change. The underlined verb "was" sounds fine in the sentence. It makes sense for the verb to be past tense. To be certain, try the other choices. All the other choices sound worse than "was."

3. Ⓑ "I **been** in organized productions since I was . . ." sounds very slangy. Try the choices. "**I had been** in organized productions since . . ." sounds great. Choices C and D don't make sense in the context of the sentence. Your ear can hear this: "I **will have been** in organized productions **since** I was . . ." doesn't sound right because it doesn't make sense; it starts in the future and ends in the past. These drills train your ear, so you can trust it.

4. Ⓓ "When I **were**" sounds weird because it doesn't match. It should be "when I **was**."

5. Ⓐ No change. "What I would say" sounds great. To be certain, try the choices, and trust your ear. Choices B, C, and D sound awkward, since they are past tense which does not fit in for the underlined words.

6. Ⓒ "What will work . . . are" sounds weird; "are" is for a group, while "what" is usually one thing. "What will work . . . is" sounds great. Choice D, "What will work . . . has been," sounds okay at first, but not with the rest of the sentence; it's talking about something that used to happen in the past, while the sentence is talking about what works all the time.

7. Ⓑ The two underlined verbs must match. "Be listening and react" sounds weird because the two verbs don't match. The verbs in choices B and C match, but only choice B sounds smooth in the sentence.

Skill 16 (page 73)

Subject/Verb Agreement Tricks

1. Stephen ~~for two more weeks~~ **is** single.

2. Margarita ~~with her sisters~~ currently **runs** a marketing firm.

3. Tricky! Running from the bulls **is** Jimmy ~~with his friends~~. ("Jimmy" is the subject.)

4. The way ~~of samurais~~ **is** a strict path.

5. Tricky! Around the corner **are** a dog and a cat. ("Dog and cat" is a compound subject.)

6. The <u>PTA</u> ~~through generous donations~~ **is** building a new school building.

7. The <u>boys</u> ~~with their dog Alfred~~ **walk** to school.

1. **C** When you see a verb underlined, ask, "What is the subject?" Cross off prepositional phrases and notice what is doing the action of the verb. It looks like "cookies **have** been" is correct, but the subject of the underlined verb "have been written" is "procedure," not "cookies," so it should be "procedure . . . ~~cookies~~ **has** been written." Your ear can hear this anyway, but now you can prove to yourself what your ear already knew.

2. **A** No change. Your ear hears that the underlined words sound good, but here's the proof. It might seem that "butter **have softened**" should be "butter **has softened**," but "butter" is not actually the subject of the underlined verb "have softened." Cross out the prepositional phrase and "sticks" is the subject: "sticks ~~of butter~~ **have softened.**"

3. **A** No change. When you see a verb underlined, ask yourself, What is the subject? Cross off prepositional phrases and notice what is doing the action of the verb. In this case, what is doing the "is-ing"? Not the "sugars," but the "one-half cup." "One-half cup ~~of brown and white sugars~~ is added." I love these, they are tricky, but we expect them and get them right!

4. **B** "Cookies" is the subject and "~~on the middle rack~~" and "~~of the oven~~" are prepositional phrases, so "becomes ready" should be "become ready." "When the **cookies,** baking ~~on the middle rack of the oven~~, become ready, . . ."

Skill 17 (page 75)

Pronoun Clarity and Agreement

1. **D** When you see a pronoun underlined, identify the noun that it refers to. "**It** is" refers to the plural "cookie cutters" and should be "**they** are."

2. **A** No change. The pronoun "them" correctly refers to "options."

3. **C** This is a great example of our most important English section strategy. Make sure to read what is really written; don't correct it in your mind. The pronoun "those" refers to "cookie cutter," but "those" is plural and "cookie cutter" is singular. So "those" should be "each." It's easy to accidentally read "cookie cutter" as "cookie cutters" to make the underlined pronoun "those" work; make sure you read what's really written and don't accidentally change something to make it correct!

4. **B** The pronoun "she" is unclear. Even though we are smart and know that the pronoun can only refer to "my grandma," technically it's not clear in the paragraph. Usually, a pronoun refers to the nearest important noun, which here would be "shapes." Ask yourself, What would an alien think if he translated this sentence? He would think that "she" refers to "shapes," so we must replace it with something clearer.

5. **A** No change. The pronoun "each" refers to "cookie" and matches perfectly. Choice C is incorrect because "this" should refer to a cookie that we are already talking about. And choice B is redundant (Skill 26 Preview); "each and every" is used in slang speech, but "every" is implied by "each" and is unneeded. The SAT always favors clear, concise, and not redundant.

6. **C** The pronoun "it" refers to "crystals" and should be the plural "they." When you see a pronoun underlined, identify the noun that it refers to. Choice D is wordy and should say "end," not "ends."

Skill 18 (page 77)

Correct Transition Word

1. **C** Trust your ear. "Otherwise" sounds weird and makes the sentence hard to understand. When you don't understand a sentence, don't say, "Well, I can't do this one." Say, "I don't

understand that, so there must be an error!" Try the choices. Choices B and D do not clear things up, but choice C makes the sentence work. The two parts of the sentence oppose each other, so the opposition word "although" works.

2. **A** No change. The transition word "though" works because the two parts of the sentence oppose each other, and "though" is an opposition word. All of the other choices are direct cause-and-effect words, not opposition words.

3. **B** "Since" is a direct cause-and-effect transition word, but the two parts of the sentence oppose each other. So "since" is wrong, and we need an opposition word. The only one in the choices is "while."

4. **D** The transition word "whereas" actually sounds fine and seems to work, until you get to the word "however" in the same sentence. The two transitions are redundant and make the sentence very confusing. "However" is not underlined, so we cannot eliminate it, and thus we must delete "whereas."

5. **A** No change. "For example" is a direct cause-and-effect word that fits well here, since the example in the sentence demonstrates the previous statement.

6. **B** Trust your ear. The transition word "therefore" sounds very awkward because it's redundant with "in truth."

Skill 19 (page 79)

Brave, Honest, and Relaxed

1. **D** The list must match: "uprooting saplings, leveling huts, and. . . ." So "disturbing animals' homes" is the best match.

2. **C** The list must match: "had been interesting, informative, and. . . ." The first two members of the list are adjectives, so the third must be too. You don't need to think of it this way; your ear can hear which one works. If it doesn't, doing these drills will train it to hear. So the answer is "had been interesting, informative, and

eye-opening." The verb "had been" is shared by all three. Either each new member has a verb, or none do; it's like bringing cupcakes to school in third grade—either you have enough for everyone or you don't bring 'em!

3. **B** The list must match: "guitarist, vocalist, drummer, and. . . ." Since the other members of the list do not have a verb, the last should not have one either. Instead, it should just be the noun "soundman" to match.

4. **C** When you have a list, all the words must match. The list is "reading comprehension questions, writing multiple-choice questions, and to write . . ." The first two parts match (they are nouns), but the fourth part, "to write," does not match. So the fourth part must also be a noun, such as "the essay."

5. **B** The list must match. Kathy feels "healthy, grounded, and. . . ." So "is ready" should just be "ready."

6. **D** The words in the list must match: "addition, multiplication, and subtraction."

Skill 20 (page 81)

Comparison

1. **A** The words that are being compared must match, and they do: "Anyone who has **extra time** or **great interest**. . . ."

2. **B** Words that are being compared must match: ". . . paint **for fun**, rather than **for profiting**. . . ." So "profiting" should just be "profit."

3. **D** Words that are being compared must match: ". . . will be known not only **as an honored graduate** . . ., but also **he writes**. . . ." So "he writes" should be "as an author" to match "as a graduate."

4. **C** Many kids will just skip this one because it's a little convoluted and weird. But it's just a comparison question. Words that are being compared must match: ". . . more on **consumer spending** than **do they rely on government subsidies**. . . ." So "than do they rely on

government subsidies" should be "than on government subsidies." The verb "rely" is used by both "consumer spending" and "government subsidies," and there is no need to repeat it before "government subsidies."

5. **D** Words that are being compared must match: "**The book**. . . . than **Karl Marx**." We can't compare a book to a person. We can compare a novel to a book or a person to a person. So "Karl Marx" should be "(a book) by Karl Marx." This seems a small, obscure, specific thing, but for some reason nearly every SAT has one of these questions on it. So expect it, and you'll get it right!

Skill 21 (page 83)

Relaxing Commas

1. **D** We don't need a pause between "room" and "is." In fact, a comma should never be sandwiched between the subject and verb of a sentence.

2. **C** Try this with and without a pause. Without a pause, the sentence gets jumbled; it incorrectly sounds as if the memories are from the three-year-old birthday poster. So which type of pause do we need? A comma is correct, since the phrase after the pause could not stand on its own. Skill 22 Preview: If it could stand on its own, then a semicolon or a comma with "and" would work.

3. **D** "The rugs underfoot being always dusty" sounds awkward. We need a pause. Choice D is correct, since "always dusty, always comforting," are side notes; they are inessential to the sentence, and therefore need commas. The "really" in choice B is slangy and unneeded, and the "are" in choice C is redundant with the "are" several words later.

4. **A** There's no need for any pauses here. Trust your ear. You can hear it.

5. **C** You can hear that we need a pause between "wall" and "blue." The phrase "blue and red" is a side note, inessential to the sentence, so we

use commas. Choice D almost works, but "being" is awkward and unneeded.

6. **D** Transition words, like "though," are usually surrounded by commas. Choice B is incorrect because it's the wrong transition, direct instead of opposition. Choice C is incorrect because we would use a semicolon only to separate two parts of a sentence that could each stand alone.

7. **B** This sentence is missing a verb, so choice B is correct.

Skill 22 (page 86)

Are You Independent?

1. **C** A comma or dash is used to separate two parts of a sentence when one of the parts could not stand alone. So choices B and D are okay, since the second part of the sentence has been changed in these choices to be dependent. A period or a semicolon is used when both parts could stand alone. Therefore, choice A works, but choice C does not, since "teaching that . . ." has no subject for the verb and could not stand alone.

2. **B** We do not need a pause here. Try it with and without a pause, and your ear can hear that we don't need one.

3. **D** We don't need a pause here. We would use a period (choice A) or a semicolon (choice B) only if both parts of the sentence could stand alone, but "and the world around them" cannot stand alone. It does not need a comma because it's not a side note, it goes with "understand themselves."

4. **A** No change. The comma is correct, since the second part of the sentence, "beginning at birth . . . ," could not stand alone.

5. **A** No change. Transition words, like "however," are usually surrounded by commas or a semicolon and a comma. We use commas if they separate a dependent clause, and we use a semicolon and a comma if they separate two independent clauses. "However" divides this sentence into two independent clauses, so "stages; however," is correct.

Skill 23 (page 89)

Correct Preposition

1. **C** "Helping out **on** Miss Kelly's study halls" sounds strange; it should be "helping out **in** Miss Kelly's study halls." That makes sense if you think about it; he literally helped "in," not "on," the study hall.

2. **B** "**In** reading" sounds weird; it should be "**to** read."

3. **A** No change. "**On** his . . . test" sounds great. The other choices sound awkward.

4. **D** "Never said a word **on** it to me" sounds very slangy; it should be "never said a word **about** it to me." This is great practice. You actually might use "word **on** it" or another of the answer choices in a slang way, but for formal use, only "about" works. That makes sense, since Nick literally spoke "about" it, not "on," "by," or "for" it.

5. **B** "Cared **for** the grade" sounds weird; it should be "cared **about** the grade."

6. **D** "**On** being" sounds weird and slangy; it should be "to be."

Skill 24 (page 91)

It's Me

1. **C** To test whether "I" is correct, just drop "Manuel." Then it reads "Sometime in college, **me** had heard," which sounds terrible, so it should be "Sometime in college, **I** had heard." Choice B does not need the comma (a comma is never sandwiched directly between a subject and a verb), and choice D is wrong because it just swapped the order of the words "Manuel" and "me."

2. **C** "Its" is possessive, and "it's" means "it is." So we need "it's," and choice C is best. Choice B also corrects the "its" problem, but it is too wordy.

3. **A** No change. "Its" is possessive, and "it's" means "it is." So we need "its," and there is no change. Also, the singular pronoun "its" correctly refers to "a yoga practice."

4. **D** To test if "I" is correct, just drop "Manuel." Then it reads "Someone brought tea to I" which sounds terrible, so it should be "Someone brought tea to **me**."

5. **C** To test if "he" is correct, just drop "his student." Then it reads "I was listening to a story about he" which sounds terrible; so it should be "I was listening to a story about him," which sounds better.

6. **A** No change. "Who" versus "whom" is probably harder for your ear to pick up, so just plug in "I" versus "me" instead of "who" versus "whom" and trust your ear. "**I** can see" sounds good, and "**me** can see" sounds terrible. Since "I" corresponds to "who" and "me" corresponds to "whom," it should read "**who** can see."

Skill 25 (page 93)

A Few More Rules

1. **A** No change. "Who" is used for people, and "which" is used for things. The "band," though composed of people, is considered a thing, so "which" is correct.

2. **C** Because we are watching for it, catching this seems ridiculously easy. But that's the key: to know that sometimes the SAT throws in an unneeded "ly." If you watch for it, these are easy!

3. **B** "They can not only deconstruct **and** also . . ." sounds awkward. "Not only" should be followed by "**but** also."

4. **A** No change. "Their" correctly refers back to "disparate pieces." Use the process of elimination. "It's" means "it is," and the other choices sound terrible.

5. **C** "Groups" is plural, so the possessive is "groups'."

Skill 26 (page 95)

Direct, to the Point, Not Redundant

1. **D** All answers besides choice D are redundant; they say the same thing twice. The SAT likes clear and concise and not redundant.

2. **C** "Stress and tension are breathed out" is passive voice. The SAT likes active voice (no offense, Yoda). Choice C is the most direct and active. Your ear can hear it; it's the most clear and direct, and the most powerful of all the choices.

3. **B** The SAT loves to use this type of question. "And less tight" basically defines "relaxed," so "relaxed, and less tight," is redundant. Choice B is the only one that corrects this.

4. **D** The underlined portion of the sentence is very wordy and muddled. Choice D is clear, direct, and concise, and it uses the active voice. Your ear can hear that it is the best choice. Also, notice that choice D is the only choice that is a direct instruction, like the rest of the passage.

5. **D** "Ready and all set" is redundant, since "all set" pretty much defines "ready." So we don't need "all set," and choice D corrects that best.

6. **D** **There's** no need to say "open your eyes and with open eyes." It's redundant. We can omit "with open eyes." You're probably pretty bored with this redundancy strategy by now, but that's great. Every SAT has several of these questions, and now you know to watch for them, and you'll get them right!

Skill 27 (page 97)

Misplaced Phrases

1. **D** The sentence makes it sound like it was "the city" that had "the fresh air of its open pasture," which makes no sense. "With the fresh air of its open pasture" should be as close to "farm" as possible, since it is describing it. So choice D is best. Seems like a picky thing? It is, but at least we know to watch for it, and we can catch it every time. If there were a million of these picky things, that'd be tough, but there are only a few.

2. **C** The sentence makes it seem that "of Rice Krispies" describes "Grandma," when of course it describes "breakfast." Choice C is the best revision. You might even be able to think up a better way to phrase it, but of the choices, C is best. Use the process of elimination; cross out choices that violate a rule, and pick the best of what is left.

3. **C** **As written**, the sentence makes it very unclear to what the descriptive phrase "in the fields baling hay" applies. It applies to "the workers," so it should be as close to them as possible. Remember, when you read a sentence and it does not make any sense, that's because it's wrong. So read the choices and see which one makes the most sense.

4. **A** No change. The sentence sounds fine, and all of the choices are wordy or have misplaced phrases. For example, choice B makes it seem that "with its familiar smell" refers to "I" rather than to "Grandpa's work shirt."

5. **B** The sentence makes it seem that "the memory" has "rhythm and simplicity" when it should be the "time I spent." Choice B is the clearest revision. Choice C sounds good at first, but "the time of the memory" does not make sense. That's a great reminder to read the whole answer choice, not just the first few words.

Skill 28 (page 99)

Word Choice

1. **C** "Demonstrates" sounds a bit strange in the sentence. Try the choices and trust your ear. Choice C sounds perfect, "The hit TV show *Entourage* **portrays** a young movie star. . . ."

2. **B** "Contests" sounds a bit strange in the sentence. Try the choices and trust your ear. Choice B sounds perfect: "the main character, Vince, faces **competition** from other actors. . . ."

3. **C** "Known to" sounds terrible in the sentence. Try the choices and trust your ear. Choice C sounds perfect: "when he was **scheduled to** go on a late night talk show. . . ."

4. **C** "Much" sounds a bit weird in the sentence. Try the choices and trust your ear. Choice C sounds perfect, "with so **many** loyal fans." In fact, "much" is used to describe something that cannot be counted or numbered, like "this much rain," and "many" is used to describe something that can be counted, like "this many **inches** of rain."

5. **B** "Inefficient" sounds a bit off in the sentence. Try the choices and trust your ear. Choice B sounds perfect: "Vince is not **indifferent**. . . ." "Indifferent" would mean that he does not care. "Absent" would not make sense, and "caring" means the opposite of what the sentence intended.

6. **A** No change. "Long shot" sounds fine in the sentence. Try the choices and trust your ear. None of the other choices sounds better.

7. **D** "Trickle" does not sound quite right in the sentence. Try the choices and trust your ear. Choice D sounds better. He pursues the long-shot because it gives him a "huge **surge**" of excitement, not a "huge trickle" or "huge tweak" of it.

Skill 29 (page 101)

Flow

1. **A** No change. The sentence as it is ties to the conclusion, since the phrase "clothing-optional" is used in both. Choice D is also in both, but it does not make sense in this sentence. These questions often confuse students until they realize that they just have to meet the **goal** stated in the question (Skill 30). Several answers look like valid substitutions for the underlined words, but only one answer meets the specific **goal** stated in the question.

2. **D** Adding the sentence "the 1970s saw an oil crisis and the growth of the environmental movement" would distract from the purpose of the paragraph. The purpose is to introduce the essay topic, which is a person's experience with his or her family's "clothing-optional" beach. So more info about the 1970s is not relevant and would be distracting in the paragraph. For a yes/no question, choose an answer that applies to the entire question and not just a few words of it.

3. **C** Each paragraph should focus on a single main idea. "I kept away" begins a new main idea, the writer returning to his or her family's beach, while the previous paragraph was about leaving the beach.

4. **D** The underlined sentence is unnecessary to the paragraph and distracts from its flow and focus.

Skill 30 (page 103)

Goal Questions

1. **C** Choice C is the one that best meets the specific **goal** of linking the first two sentences, birth to nickname. Choice A mentions Anacostia but is not a complete sentence.

2. **B** All of the sentences are interesting and would add to the paragraph, but only choice B meets the specific **goal** to "briefly describe the content of the autobiography." These questions often confuse students until they realize that they have to meet the **goal** stated in the question. Several of the answers look valid, but there's only one answer that meets the **goal.**

3. **C** Choices B, C, and D are all good conclusions. But choice C best meets the **goal** to "maintain the tone established in the introduction," since it refers to the language of the intro with "Sage of Anacostia." Choice B is second-best, but it has no direct reference to the introduction.

Skill 31 (page 105)

Yes or No?

1. **D** The essay does not summarize "the curriculum at the top three schools." The essay just provides a general overview. Yes/no questions are a type of goal question, and we need to meet the specific goal stated in the question. Make sure to choose an answer that applies to the entire question and not just a few words of it. Choice C is incorrect because the passage says that we know "little"—not "almost nothing"—about their training; the third paragraph mentions what we do know about their training, but does not mention "the top three schools."

2. **C** The statement "The truth is that" is redundant. The writer would not make a statement in this kind of factual essay unless it were true, so we do not need "The truth is that."

3. **C** A conclusion should wrap up an essay and bring some closure. It might restate the thesis or main idea of the essay, it might use language that reminds us of the introduction, or it might recap the main points of the essay. This paragraph does none of these and is not a conclusion.

Skill 32 (page 107)

Adverbs End in 'ly"

1. **D** Easy, if you know to watch for it! It should be "understanding this article **correctly.**"

2. **D** The trucks "passed **constantly,**" not "**constant.**"

3. **D** His feet brought him places "**slowly**" not "**slow.**" The other answer choices violate parallel structure and obscure the meaning of the sentence.

4. **A** No error. "**Quickly**" sounds correct and is correct.

5. **D** The tourist is trying "**desperately,**" not "**desperate,**" to communicate. Other choices

either sound terrible or obscure the meaning of the sentence.

6. **C** "Promotes healing more **quick**" should be "promotes healing more **quickly.**"

Skill 33 (page 109)

Jedi Master Yoda

1. **D** "Passing . . . is what Juana did" is passive and wordy. Choice D, "Juana passed," is active and direct.

2. **C** The whole sentence is wordy, indirect, passive, and confusing. Choice C is more active and direct. To make this "hard" question easier, use the process of elimination. Most of the choices are crazy and confusing. Trust your ear. If you can't even understand what a sentence is saying, then it's not written well—eliminate it as a choice!

3. **B** "Learning . . . is the reason that" is passive and wordy. Choice B is more direct and clear. To make this "hard" question easier, use the process of elimination. Most of the choices are crazy and confusing. Trust your ear. If you can't even understand what a sentence is saying, then it's not written well—eliminate it as a choice!

4. **D** "Five is the number he counted to" is passive and wordy. (Bad grammar, Brother Maynard!) Choice D is direct and clear. To make this "hard" question easier, use the process of elimination.

Skill 34 (page 111)

Combining Sentences

1. **B** You can see that this is simply a combination of several Skills. The reproduced sentences are not too bad, but the question asks us to combine them. That makes sense, since the SAT loves conciseness. To find the correct answer, use the process of elimination. You know from Skill 27 that choice A makes it seem that the "lucid explanations" are the instructor, a

misplaced descriptive phrase. Choice C sounds wordy and awkward. Choice D needs a semicolon instead of a comma, since both parts could stand alone. Choice B is best. It is clear and direct.

2. **D** Choice D is the most clear, direct, and concise revision.

3. **A** "The book has many interesting characters" is a nice transition into the next two paragraphs, which look at specific characters.

4. **C** "Next, there's Harry Potter" introduces the third paragraph, which is primarily about Harry Potter.

5. **A** A concluding sentence for the essay should sum up the whole essay—its main idea. Several of the sentences are interesting, but choice A best sums up the main idea of the passage.

Skill 35 (page 114)

How to Think Like a Grammar Genius

1. **C** "Well known" defines "famous," so "famous well known" is redundant. Choice C, deleting "well known," is the best correction.

2. **C** "Different times **of** history" sounds weird. Try each choice and trust your ear. "Different times **in** history" sounds great. The "times" are literally **in**, not **of**, history. Choice D is too slangy.

3. **D** The word "originally" and the verb "married" tell us that the sentence relates to the past, so the underlined verbs should also be past tense: "lived . . . and depended." The other choices are not past tense.

4. **B** Try this one with and without the pause. No pause sounds strange, jumbled, and rushed. We need a comma after "easier." We use a comma, not a semicolon, since the first part of the sentence is dependent.

5. **B** The "its" used here means "it is" and should be "it's." Remember that "its" is possessive, like "a bear defends its cubs."

6. **A** No change. Most people find it very hard to hear when "who" or "whom" is correct, so we make it easy and use "I" versus "me" instead. "I" corresponds to "who" and "me" corresponds to "whom." In this sentence, "I complete them" sounds fine, and "me complete them" sounds weird. So "I" is correct, which means that "who" is correct. Notice that choice D is not correct, since "which" is used with things and "who" or "whom" is used with people.

7. **C** The clause "the person that makes them feel at ease" is dependent—it could not stand alone. It leaves you waiting for the action. Choice C is correct. Choices A and B are incorrect because a period or semicolon is used to separate two independent clauses that could stand alone. Choice D is incorrect because, without a pause, the sentence sounds jumbled.

Essay

Skill 36 (page 117)

Reading

Answers will vary. Hold your pencil as you read and note any evidence, reasoning, and stylistic devices that you notice.

Skill 37 (page 121)

Prove It!

Answers will vary. Your answer should address the following questions. Is the author's evidence relevant to his argument? Is it powerful and compelling? Does it come from impressive, credible sources? Does the author smoothly link the evidence to his claims? What is the author's flow of reasoning? Does A lead to B and connect to C?

Skill 38 (page 123)

Dude's Got Style

Answers will vary. What stylistic devices did the author use to persuade the reader?

Skill 39 (page 125)

Craft Your Thesis

Answers will vary. Look over the evidence, reasoning, and stylistic devices that you have circled or underlined and craft your thesis. Your thesis should list the main ideas of your body paragraphs. One of my students, Sarah, wrote the following:

> In the passage, King persuasively argues that the United States' involvement in the war is unjust; King stakes this claim through skillful word choice which appeals to the emotions of his audience, by establishing his own credibility, and through his logical sequence of ideas.

Skill 40 (page 127)

Intro Paragraph

Answers will vary. Does your intro paragraph have an opener, a link, and a thesis?

Here's what Sarah wrote:

> Can a civil rights leader also be a pacifist? In Martin Luther King, Jr.'s "Beyond Vietnam—A Time to Break Silence," King says yes. In the passage, King persuasively argues that the United States' involvement in the war is unjust; King stakes this claim through skillful word choice which appeals to the emotions of his audience, by establishing his own credibility, and through his logical sequence of ideas.

Skill 41 (page 129)

Transition Sentences

Answers will vary. Use transition sentences to begin each paragraph, link it to the previous paragraph, and/or remind the reader of your thesis.

Sarah used this transition into her first body paragraph, "Martin Luther King, Jr.'s choice of diction provokes emotion from his audience." It's short, but it's clear and it gets the job done.

Skill 42 (page 131)

Body Paragraph I

Answers will vary. Is your body paragraph written around a single main idea? Is it jam packed with supporting details?

Here is Sarah's body paragraph:

> Martin Luther King, Jr.'s choice of diction provokes emotion from his audience. For example, when addressing the loss of lives due to the war, he specifically mentions "sons," "brothers," and "husbands" who were sent to "fight and to die." The use of the words "sons," "brothers," and "husbands" will make the audience think of their own families. By evoking this thought of families, King brings out the protective nature of most humans in regard to their own families. Thusly, King makes his audience want to protect those who are being sent to war. In another example of effective word choice, when he is speaking of the damage being done to America, King states, "If America's soul becomes totally poisoned, part of the autopsy must read: Vietnam." The word "autopsy" is often associated with death and even, on television and in the media, with death by foul play. King's use of this term not only incites a sense of fear in his audience and implies that America is in danger, but also suggests that there is something illegal or unjust at the root of the danger. This supports King's main point that the war is unjust and is putting America in danger. Throughout the essay, King's expert use of diction brings out emotion in his audience.

Sarah hit a home run with details, analysis, and depth. The paragraph centers around diction and uses two powerful examples from the passage to demonstrate her point. Graders love that she went deep in her analysis of the connotations of the word *autopsy*, even looking at the criminal implications King's audience will have with the word.

Skill 43 (page 133)

Body Paragraph II

Answers will vary. Does your next body paragraph (or two) continue demonstrating your thesis? Is it focused on a specific example mentioned in your thesis? Does it begin with a transition sentence that smoothly links it to the previous body paragraph?

Here's Sarah's next body paragraph:

> King begins his speech with the phrase "Since I am a preacher," which establishes his own credibility. The position of a preacher is normally one that commands respect. A preacher is expected to hold

183

high moral standards and act for the greater good of the people. By establishing himself as a preacher, he is also establishing that his argument is being made with good intentions. Another way that King establishes his credibility is by explaining that one of the reasons for his beliefs stems from "[his] experience in the ghettos." By informing his audience that he has witnessed an issue first hand and personally interacted with those who have been affected, he is connecting with his audience and assuring them of the validity of his argument. King greatly strengthens his argument through these examples of establishing his credibility.

Great paragraph! Nice transition, good evidence from the passage, effective analysis. Yes, Sarah is brilliant and has a great mind for analysis, but you can do it too; these drills teach you to do what she did!

Skill 44 (page 135)

A Strong Body

Sarah's next body paragraph examines the third point in her thesis, that King uses logical sequencing of his ideas to bring the reader to the conclusion that the war is unjust.

> By logically sequencing his ideas, King is able to effectively persuade the audience of his point. King first explains the background of the issue. He explains that before the war, poverty programs were developing and there were "experiments, hopes, new beginnings." He then explains that the war has put a stop to this progress being made in America as funds and energy are channeled to the war; he establishes the war as the "enemy of the poor." Furthermore, he realizes that the poor are losing their lives in the war in disproportionately high numbers. He asks how can we send our boys to death for freedom in Asia when they don't have this very freedom at home in Georgia? These points appeal to the emotion of his audience, bringing out fear and anger, which allows him to effectively direct this negative emotion towards the government, "the greatest purveyor of violence." Through this logical sequence of ideas, King effectively leads his audience to the realization that the war is unjust and that the government is the perpetrator.

Skill 45 (page 137)

What's the Problem?

If you have time, add a paragraph about things that the author might have improved. Did you notice anything that King could have done more effectively? Is there evidence that you might have liked to see? Did he miss out on making a point? If so, this makes a great paragraph and adds definite points to your essay.

Skill 46 (page 139)

Stretch the Dough

Were you able to lengthen your paragraph? The College Board has made one thing very clear: How much you write matters. You can reference another piece of evidence from the passage. Or explain more clearly how a citation from the passage was effective. Analyze deeper. Go out on a limb. Remember how Tavi made the leap about the effective psychology of Lev's rhetorical questions. Expand more on whatever you just wrote. Explain your thinking more clearly. Speculate on why an author chose a certain logic or style. Whatever you are writing about, write more about that.

Skill 47 (page 141)

Conclusion

Answers will vary. Does your conclusion restate your thesis, link, and end with a bang? Remember, I'm not telling you to be boring or predictable. Use this as a framework and build your own masterpiece around it.

Here's Sarah's conclusion:

> Through his choice of diction, establishment of credibility, and logical sequence of ideas, Martin Luther King, Jr. is able to effectively persuade his audience that the war in Vietnam is unjust.

Sarah was running out of time, so she threw down only one sentence, but the sentence accomplishes the task. (Most important, there must be a conclusion of some kind if you are to get full credit.) Even just one sentence can wrap up the essay and brings it full circle back to the thesis.

Skill 48 (page 143)

Other Stuff That Matters

1. "Immutable" means "unchanging" or "indisputable."
Example: Death and taxes are immutable truths.

"Eradicated" means "erased completely."
Example: Vaccines have nearly eradicated polio.

"Auspicious" means "fortunate" or "lucky."
Example: The French interest in a Northern victory proved auspicious for Lincoln.

"Superfluous" means "unneeded" or "inessential."
Example: Critics state that the government overspends on superfluous items.

"Affinity" means "liking" or "inclination."
Example: Gatsby was known for his large parties, yet he had an affinity for privacy.

"Concordant" means "in agreement."
Example: The ideas expressed in Lincoln's speech were concordant with his earlier declarations.

"Pertinent" means "relevant."
Example: Gandhi's way of life is pertinent if we want to understand his politics.

"Thwart" means "to prevent."
Example: The storm thwarted the thief's plan.

"Ramification" means "effect."
Example : There were many ramifications of the Civil War.

2. Answers will vary. In your paragraph, did you go deep, write a fair bit, use some impressive vocab, vary your sentences, write readably, and avoid basic grammar and spelling errors?

Skill 49 (page 145)

Proofread

Answers will vary. Proofread for omitted words, misspellings, and punctuation errors, and to make sure that you indented new paragraphs when you meant to and wrote details correctly.

Skill 50 (page 147)

How to Be a Writing Monster

Answers will vary. Did you use the Skills? Check your essay, item by item, with this checklist. Check off items that you have mastered, and circle items that still need improvement.

☐ **Skill 36.** Read the passage twice. While you are reading, hold your pencil and underline, circle, or make notes in the margin when you see evidence, reasoning, and stylistic devices.

☐ **Skill 37.** Think about the relevance and reliability of the author's evidence. Also consider the author's use of logical reasoning to connect that evidence to the argument. Does A lead to B and connect to C?

☐ **Skill 38.** As you read the passage, watch for *stylistic or persuasive elements, such as word choice or appeals to emotion, to add power to the ideas expressed.* This might include descriptive detail that engages the reader, presenting a personal anecdote, asking rhetorical questions, using certain loaded words, or inspiring emotion in the reader.

☐ **Skill 39.** Look over the evidence, reasoning, and stylistic devices that you circled or underlined and craft your thesis. This is the outline for the body paragraphs of the essay.

☐ **Skill 40.** Your intro paragraph should be 3 to 5 sentences: an opener, a link, and a thesis.

☐ **Skill 41.** Use transition sentences to begin each paragraph, link it to the previous paragraph, and/or remind the reader of your thesis.

☐ **Skill 42.** Begin each "body" paragraph with a link to the previous paragraph, and write each around a single main idea.

☐ **Skill 43.** The next body paragraph(s) should address the second point in your thesis. It should be organized around a specific main idea. Ideally, it should link smoothly to your previous body paragraph(s).

☐ **Skill 44.** Support your generalizations with relevant paraphrases and quotations from the passage.

☐ **Skill 45.** If you have time, add a paragraph about what the author might have improved.

☐ **Skill 46.** Write more.

☐ **Skill 47.** Structure your conclusion by restating your thesis, linking, and ending with a bang.

☐ **Skill 48.** In your essay, go deep, write 3 pages at the very least, use some impressive vocab, vary your sentences, write readably, and avoid basic grammar and spelling errors.

☐ **Skill 49.** Leave a few minutes to proofread your essay for omitted words, misspellings, and punctuation errors, and to make sure that you have represented details accurately and started new paragraphs where you meant to by indenting.

The more details, depth of analysis, and cool vocab you include, the higher your score will be.

Posttest I (page 152)

1. Ⓑ Always begin a reading passage by reading the intro paragraph; in this passage, the author is "exploring his heritage." This is confirmed throughout the passage. So, let's use the process of elimination, looking for words related to "exploring his heritage."

   Ⓐ persuade—No, he is not persuading us.

   Ⓑ inform—Yes.

   Ⓒ apologize—No.

   Ⓓ eulogize—No; he respects his grandparents, but it's not a eulogy.

   This is a great example of why the process of elimination is so great. I might not have looked for the answer "inform," but it is certainly the best of the choices and the correct answer.

2. Ⓓ The answer should be in the lines referred to or soon after them. In this case, the answer comes in the next two sentences; the author

considers Judaism, rather than being Austrian, to be part of his heritage. Choice D is the best answer.

3. Ⓑ To answer a "most nearly means" question, reread a few lines before and a few lines after. "**While** my mother's . . . , my paternal . . . " indicates that "paternal" is the opposite of "mother's," so it is "father's." The word "while" indicates that the two parts of the sentence are in opposition.

4. Ⓒ The answers are in the sentences following the line referred to. The sentences tell us that "he completed high school, college, and graduate degrees . . . worked as a principal . . . was a talented teacher." Choice C, "prone to worry," is mentioned in the passage, but not as evidence of his being an "academic."

   For a "direct info" question, always read before and after a line and find proof. Sometimes you need to read even more for an EXCEPT question; so if you are pressed for time, you can skip EXCEPT questions and come back to them. Sometimes they're easy, and at other times they're like four questions in one and you have to search the whole passage for info.

5. Ⓑ The answer comes in the previous part of the sentence. Even though Judaism is a large part of the narrator's identity, he rarely thinks of it and does not observe holidays. Be careful of choice C, which is mentioned, but which has nothing to do with the question. The answer to a "suggest" question is often a rewording of something in the passage, and is rarely a direct quote, like choice C. For "suggest" questions, look for the answer that is hinted at in the passage. Though it might have different language, it should be pretty close to what is actually said.

6. Ⓓ Since the italics state that the passage is from a scientific paper that explores water resources, we can assume that it will be scientific—in other words, that it will be unbiased, detached, and analytical.

7. **C** The author's tone in the first sentence is reflected by the language: "The city of Meadville is particularly well blessed in terms of water resources." The tone is analytical and almost enthusiastic. Use the process of elimination. It is not choice B or D, "contemptuous" (disapproving) or "mischievous." Choice A, "joyous," is too extreme. And even though the writer uses the phrase "well blessed," the tone is not solemn (somber). Choice C, "diagnostic," is best.

8. **A** We definitely want to use the process of elimination here. It might be initially tough to come up with a difference between the two paragraphs, but going through the choices shows that only choice A even remotely makes sense. The third paragraph tells about precipitation, which is mentioned only briefly in the second paragraph. The other choices do not work because there is no time order, no emotion, and no fiction. Remember, don't get intimidated. Stay with it and give it a try, and sometimes, like on this question, you will get one right that you thought you had no chance on!

9. **D** If you need help with the main idea, reread the first and last lines of the paragraph. The final paragraph explores precipitation **replenishing** the water supply. This is demonstrated clearly in the first and last lines of the paragraph.

This question is another great reminder that you should read the whole answer and not just pick a choice based on the first few words. For example, the first few words of choice A look great, but the last few are clearly not related to the paragraph—there was no mention of a shortage.

Answering questions based on the first few words alone is the most common careless error that I see on the reading section.

10. **C** Lines 28–30, "French . . . significantly," provides the best evidence for the answer to the previous question.

11. **A** The passage states that "the outwash aquifers exist mainly in the valleys and produce far better yields, since the thick drifts of sand and gravel are far more permeable."

12. **C** Generally parentheses are used to include information that is interesting but inessential or to indicate a side comment to the reader. Choice C describes this best.

13. **B** For a "parallel" question, don't get thrown if the choices are not from the passage. Stay relaxed and focused, and look for the choice that proves or disproves the statement. In this case, the question asks which choice will enter the system promptly. Rain falling on the area will enter fastest. Even for a "parallel" question, we want proof in the passage, and choice B has the most proof. Choice C will enter, but later, as mentioned in the next line of the passage.

14. **C** The passage is primarily an unemotional account of the water system.

15. **C** When a verb is underlined, trust your ear. "I have been waking" sounds weird after "one day last year." That's because "last year" is done and tells us that "have been waking" should be "woke."

16. **D** When a verb is underlined, identify the subject and cross out any prepositional phrases; a prepositional phrase NEVER counts as the subject of the verb. "With no results" is a prepositional phrase. So "she" is the subject of the underlined verb, and "she **were** trying" should be "she **was** trying."

17. **D** When a pronoun is underlined, we must be totally sure what noun it is referring to. If this is unclear in any way, it is incorrect. The underlined pronoun must also match (singular or plural) the noun that it refers to. We can't tell whether the underlined "she" refers to Jenna or Sapphire. Use the process of elimination. The only answer that corrects the problem is choice B.

18. **B** If a transition word (such as "although," "since," "but," "therefore," or "however") is underlined, see if it works in the flow of the

paragraph. "Therefore" implies cause and effect and does not fit into the flow. The sentences are not cause and effect, but in chronological order, so the answer is choice B, "Then." You can also use the process of elimination and see which choice sounds best in the flow of the sentences. Your ear will know!

19. **B** Items in a list must match. The list is "would the bat attack her, would it hide, or . . . ," so the third item should start with "would."

20. **A** Items being compared must match. We can compare Jenna and the bat (both living things), but not the bat and Jenna's skills (choice D). Choice B is slangy, and the verb in choice C doesn't match the verb that goes with the bat.

21. **C** We never need a comma right between a subject "I" and a verb "sat." The comma after "sat" works because "anxiously watching Jenna" is a side note. You can hear the pause when you read it. Also, without the comma, it would seem that "anxiously" describes the way they sat.

22. **A** "About the shots to come" could not stand alone, so we separate the clauses with commas, not a semicolon. Also, in this case, "however" is a side note and is separated with commas.

23. **B** When a preposition is underlined, ask yourself if it is the right preposition to use. "Woken up **about** a bat" sounds weird. Literally, she "woke up **with** a bat in her room." She did not literally "wake up **from** a bat in her room." That's too slangy.

24. **A** "It's" means "it is," and "its" is possessive, like "that tree is nice; I like its colorful leaves." So "It's" is correct in this sentence. "It's" does not sound terrific in this sentence, but using the process of elimination, it's the best choice.

25. **D** The nurses are not possessing anything, so we do not need the apostrophe s ('s). If one nurse had possessed something, we'd use "nurse's," and if more than one had possessed it, we'd use "nurses'."

26. **D** The SAT likes crisp and clear; we always want the answer that is most clear, concise, direct, and nonredundant. "Have to be getting" is very wordy. Choice D is clearest and most direct.

27. **A** A descriptive phrase on the SAT must be clearly associated with (and usually placed right next to) the noun described. Choice A is correct because the phrase "having trouble finding my vein" is correctly associated with (and next to) "the nurse," whom it describes. It was not "I" (choice B) or "were" (choice C) that was "having trouble finding my vein," and choice D is wordy and passive.

28. **C** Make sure that the underlined word fits in the context of the sentence. She was not waiting "greatly," "deeply," or "intensely (powerfully)." She was waiting "anxiously."

29. **C** For "flow" questions, use the process of elimination. The underlined portion is hilarious! If it were cut, the passage would lose "a comical anecdote (a funny story)." The underlined portion is not a tie-in to the introduction or a transition.

30. **A** For "goal" questions, choose the one answer choice that achieves the very specific GOAL stated in the question. The very specific goal for this question is to "best introduce the tone and focus of the paragraph." The focus of the paragraph is her nickname, "rabies girl." So choice A is best. All of the other choices are relevant to the passage, but **only** choice A is relevant to that paragraph.

31. **B** A conclusion wraps up an essay. The final paragraph of this passage is a successful conclusion. It wraps up her rabies experience and even offers a lesson that she learned.

32. **C** In this sentence, "invincible" is an adjective, so it does not need an "ly."

33. **B** Choice B is active voice.

34. **A** "And I could go up to any animal I wanted without getting rabies" combines the sentences

best. Choice B is incorrect, since "therefore" does not makes sense. Choice C needs a semi-colon rather than a comma, and choice D is crazy.

35. **C** Use your ear to test the underlined verb. "Today I was felt" sounds strange. Use the process of elimination. Only choice C sounds better, and the underlined verb "was felt" should be "feel." Choice D almost works, but it is too slangy; it should be "**have** been feeling."

36–50. Did you use the Skills? Check your essay, item by item, with this checklist.

If you don't feel confident checking your own essay, ask a friend, parent, or teacher to use the list. Check off items that you mastered, and circle items that need improvement.

☐ **Skill 35.** Read the passage twice. While you read, hold your pencil and underline, circle, or make notes in the margin when you see evidence, reasoning, and stylistic devices.

☐ **Skill 36.** Think about the relevance and reliability of the author's evidence. Also consider the author's use of logical reasoning to connect that evidence to the argument. Does A lead to B and connect to C?

☐ **Skill 37.** As you read the passage, watch for *stylistic or persuasive elements, such as word choice or appeals to emotion, to add power to the ideas expressed.* This might include descriptive detail that engages the reader, presenting a personal anecdote, asking rhetorical questions, using certain loaded words, or inspiring emotion in the reader.

☐ **Skill 38.** Look over the evidence, reasoning, and stylistic devices that you circled or underlined

and craft your thesis. This is the outline for the body paragraphs of the essay.

☐ **Skill 39.** Your intro paragraph should be 3 to 5 sentences: an opener, a link, and a thesis.

☐ **Skill 40.** Use transition sentences to begin each paragraph, link it to the previous paragraph, and/or remind the reader of your thesis.

☐ **Skill 41.** Begin each "body" paragraph with a link to the previous paragraph, and write each around a single main idea.

☐ **Skill 42.** The next body paragraph(s) should address the second point in your thesis. It should be organized around a specific main idea. Ideally, it smoothly links to your previous body paragraph(s).

☐ **Skill 43.** Support your generalizations with relevant paraphrases and quotations from the passage.

☐ **Skill 44.** If you have time, add a paragraph about what the author might have improved.

☐ **Skill 45.** Write more.

☐ **Skill 46.** Structure your conclusion by restating your thesis, linking, and ending with a bang.

☐ **Skill 47.** In your essay, get deep, write at least 3 pages, use some impressive vocab, vary your sentences, write readably, and avoid basic grammar and spelling errors.

☐ **Skill 48.** Leave a few minutes to proofread your essay for omitted words, misspellings, and punctuation errors, and to make sure that you represented details accurately and started new paragraphs where you meant to by indenting.

BONUS Question.   B

Notes